More Tips for Tops

More Tips for Tops

by
Dr. George Rosenkranz

Foreword by Bobby Wolff

**Published by
Devyn Press, Inc.
Louisville, Kentucky**

To my beloved family, and especially
to its two youngest members,
Tamara and Adrian,
who I hope one day will be
attracted to my favorite hobby.

OTHER BOOKS BY GEORGE ROSENKRANZ

Bridge — The Bidder's Game

Everything You Always Wanted to Know About Trump Leads

Tips for Tops

Modern Ideas in Bidding — Revised Edition
(with Alan Truscott)

Bid to Win, Play for Pleasure
(with Phillip Alder)

Devyn Press, Inc.
3600 Chamberlain Lane, Suite 230,
Louisville, KY 40241

ISBN 0-910791-85-6

Table of Contents

Section C — Declarer-Play

Section D — General

Acknowledgments

I would like to express my thanks to the many people who have helped with the preparation of this book:

The American Contract Bridge League for its permission to use articles originally published in the *Bulletin*.

My wife, Edith, for her constant encouragement and support. She reads all my articles and has made innumerable useful suggestions and improvements.

Eddie Wold for his countless constructive comments and continuous motivation.

Marinesa Letizia, Mike Passell and Paul Soloway for hands they have given to me, and for their suggestions for Tips.

Beatriz Coarasa and Lyn Balfour for hard work, long hours and unfailing assistance in the preparation of some of the material for this book.

Phillip Alder for his invaluable help in editing and type-setting the manuscript. We have spent many pleasurable hours discussing all aspects of bridge (and other subjects of mutual interest). During these conversations he has provided much food for thought both for new Tips and for technical improvements to Tips already in production.

George Rosenkranz

Foreword

Writing an introduction for George Rosenkranz's latest book, *More Tips for Tops*, brings back fond memories. An unforgettable bridge thrill occurred with George as one of my partners and team-mates. In the 1967 Spingold in Montreal, although finishing second, we qualified for the International Trials for the first time. Thank you, George, for your expertise and contributions in that event.

Now all bridge players can thank you for putting together a clear, practical description of what it takes to win at bridge. *More Tips for Tops* covers many aspects of bridge in the trenches. From opening leads to bidding judgment to practical declarer's play to partnership defense to psychological insight, George has included all the important aspects of our game. If you love bridge and cherish winning, read and follow George's tips. *He's been there!*

Bobby Wolff

Introduction

If we offend, it is with our good will.
That you should think, we come not to offend,
But with good will. To show our simple skill,
That is the true beginning of our end.
Consider then we come but in despite.
We do not come as minding to content you,
Our true intent is. All for your delight.

Much Ado About Nothing, *William Shakespeare*

With only 52 pieces of paste-board and a vocabulary of fifteen words, it amazes me how much enjoyment we derive from bridge, and how many newspaper columns, magazines and books are published about the game.

I have tried to do my part to contribute to the production of these printed words. Reading in itself is an admirable activity. Also, we should strive to learn more — and I try to expand the bridge knowledge of my readers.

This new book, *More Tips for Tops*, has been divided into four sections. The first three are devoted to the different aspects of the game: bidding, defense and declarer-play. The last part is of a more general nature covering ideas rarely if ever seen in print.

To give you a chance to exercise your own imaginations, the first three sections begin with a quiz. Assume that each question comes from an imp match unless told otherwise, so that overtricks are relatively unimportant. Answer the problems, then read the subsequent chapters to learn my suggested solutions. After that, discuss my ideas with your partner and adopt those that appeal to you. I'm sure you won't agree with everything I say — but that is another reason for bridge's success: there are always several ways to try to solve the same problem.

Good luck at and away from the bridge table.

George Rosenkranz

Section A

Bidding

The Prologue

What's past is prologue.

The Tempest, *William Shakespeare*

1. Dlr: East
Vul: None

♠ A 3
♡ Q 8 7 5
◇ J 9 8 7 5 4
♣ 9

♠ K 10
♡ A J 6 4 3
◇ A 6
♣ Q 6 5 2

You reach four hearts, West having overcalled one spade. West leads the king of clubs and switches to a low spade. What is your plan of campaign?

(Page 8)

2. Dlr: West
Vul: N-S

♠ 7
♡ A 9 7 5 3
◇ 9 8 4
♣ K J 6 2

♠ K Q
♡ 10
◇ A Q J 7 6 5
♣ A 9 8 4

West	North	East	South
1♠	Pass	1NT (a)	3◇ (b)
4♠	5◇	Dble	Pass
Pass	Pass		

(a) Not forcing
(b) Not weak!

West leads the ace of spades and switches to the two of hearts. How do you continue?

(Page 9)

3. Dlr: South   ♠ J 4
Vul: Both   ♡ A Q 9 2
                      ♢ A K 6 5
                      ♣ 5 4 3

                      ♠ A K 10 9 8
                      ♡ 10 8
                      ♢ 2
                      ♣ A K J 8 7

You reach six clubs, promptly doubled by West. The opening lead is the jack of diamonds; how do you play to bring home your slam?

(Page 10)

4. Playing in a pair event and sitting North with both sides vulnerable, you pick up:

    ♠ 5 ♡ 8 3 ♢ J 10 9 8 7 4 ♣ A J 7 3

Your partner opens one diamond and the next player overcalls one spade. How do you plan the auction?

(Page 18)

5. Once more you are North with both sides vulnerable. This is your hand:

    ♠ J 9 3 2 ♡ K 10 7 5 ♢ Q 9 4 ♣ K 7

The auction starts like this:

West	North	East	South
			1♡
Pass	2♡	Pass	Pass
2NT (a)	?		

(a) Minor two-suiter

What would you do now? Does it matter if it is matchpoints or imps?

(Page 24)

6. With only your side vulnerable, you, West, pick up:

♠ A K Q 9   ♡ K 4   ◇ A J 10 7   ♣ A Q 4

The bidding begins as follows:

West	North	East	South
			Pass
2♣	Pass	2◇	3♣
?			

Given that it is matchpoints, what action would you take?

(Page 28)

7. With both sides vulnerable, you are West clutching:

♠ Q J 10 3   ♡ 2   ◇ J 10 9 7 5   ♣ J 6 2

The bidding proceeds:

West	North	East	South
			1♡
Pass	4◇ (a)	Pass	4♡
Pass	Pass	Pass	

(a) Splinter bid

What is your lead? What would you lead if your partner doubled the four-diamond splinter bid?

(Page 41)

Chapter 1

Leave Advertising to Madison Avenue

*Freedom of the press in Britain is freedom to print such of the
proprietor's prejudices as the advertisers don't object to.*

Hannen Swaffer

In past articles, I have repeatedly stressed the importance of
Thomas Carlyle's dictum: Speech is silvern, but silence is golden.

Unfortunately, the parrot syndrome is too deeply ingrained in
the habits of the common bridge player (*Ludus competitor vulgaris*).

A special case of this ailment — and one that runs to epidemic
proportions — is the penalty double of the opponents' suit contract.
Be honest, how often did you double on a trump stack, only to see
the tables turned on you with the declarer either fulfilling his
contract or going one down instead of finishing two or more down
undoubled?

At imps or rubber bridge, there is hardly any excuse for this
course of action, particularly against non-vulnerable opponents.

Now let us pause for a moment and consider the definition of
a trump stack. Q 10 8 5 2 in front of the declarer may produce fewer
tricks than you wishfully think. Even sitting behind the declarer, you
may be endplayed and forced to lead into declarer's tenace. The
right holding for doubling is one that contains *sure* trump tricks like
Q J 10 9 7 or J 10 9 8 2. Also, it can prove effective to double for
penalties when you know the opponents have run into a misfit.

In other words, double for penalties when you *know* that your
holding represents a disagreeable surprise for declarer — and one
about which he can do nothing, either in this contract *or* in any
other contract he might move to when warned about the impending
fate of his present one.

Playing matchpoints, the story is somewhat different. Close
doubles are the trademark of the successful duplicate player. When
your side can score, say, 140 in three hearts, you must either double
three spades for 200 or 300 rather than accept a lesser penalty, or
sacrifice for minus 100 in four hearts if you think three spades will

make and you are non-vulnerable. But never forget that you are still wielding a two-edged sword and the risk is all yours. On the one hand, you are trying for a big magic plus score, but at the same time a good declarer will use to his advantage the information your double conveys.

The following three hands are eloquent illustrations of this theme. The first occurred during the 1979 European Championships in Lausanne, Switzerland.

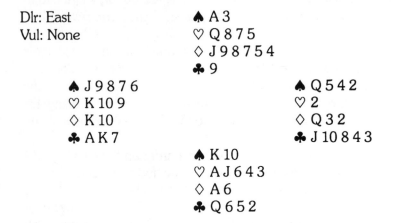

Dlr: East
Vul: None

♠ A 3
♡ Q 8 7 5
◇ J 9 8 7 5 4
♣ 9

♠ J 9 8 7 6   ♠ Q 5 4 2
♡ K 10 9   ♡ 2
◇ K 10   ◇ Q 3 2
♣ A K 7   ♣ J 10 8 4 3

♠ K 10
♡ A J 6 4 3
◇ A 6
♣ Q 6 5 2

Both declarers were in four hearts; both Wests led a top club and switched to a spade.

Claude Rodrigue, for Great Britain, had been doubled by West. He won trick two in hand and continued with the ace and another heart. West rose with the king and played a second spade, but declarer switched his attention to diamonds, eventually ruffing the third round with the jack of hearts. Plus 590.

Lorenzo Lauria, for Italy, was not doubled. He won trick two in the dummy and led a heart to the jack. He could no longer make the contract. When he tried to establish the diamonds, Lauria walked into a trump promotion. Twelve imps to Great Britain.

The second deal took place in England, also in 1979.

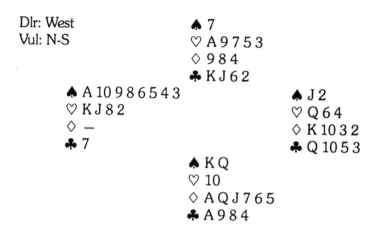

Dlr: West
Vul: N-S

```
                        ♠ 7
                        ♡ A 9 7 5 3
                        ◇ 9 8 4
                        ♣ K J 6 2
♠ A 10 9 8 6 5 4 3                         ♠ J 2
♡ K J 8 2                                  ♡ Q 6 4
◇ —                                        ◇ K 10 3 2
♣ 7                                        ♣ Q 10 5 3
                        ♠ K Q
                        ♡ 10
                        ◇ A Q J 7 6 5
                        ♣ A 9 8 4
```

In one room, West opened four spades and all passed. North did well in that he started with the ace and another heart. However, for some bizarre reason, South discarded! Declarer played two rounds of trumps and claimed.

Our attention, though, is centered on the other table. The auction went like this:

West	North	East	South
1♠	Pass	1NT (a)	3◇ (b)
4♠	5◇	Dble	Pass
Pass	Pass		

(a) Not forcing
(b) Not weak!

West led the ace of spades and switched to the two of hearts. Declarer won in the dummy and, warned by the double, ran the nine of diamonds.[1] Next, the eight of diamonds was covered by the ten and queen.

Declarer stopped to consider the lie of the hand. From the bidding and trick-two switch, West seemed to have started with 8-4-0-1 distribution. To confirm this assessment, declarer cashed the queen of spades. The appearance of the jack was gratifying.

---

[1] True, without the double he might have found this play anyway, but it is less likely.

Declarer needed to be able to make three club tricks, plus have a dummy entry to pick up the king of diamonds. This would be relatively easy if West's club were the ten or queen, but South showed that the singleton seven was sufficient. At trick six, declarer led the *nine* of clubs and ran it to East's ten.

The heart switch was ruffed, and dummy entered by leading the *eight* of clubs to the king. The jack of clubs was covered by the queen and king, but dummy could be reentered in clubs, the carefully preserved four being overtaken by the six while East followed impotently with the five!

The diamond finesse was taken and plus 750 (and fifteen imps) written on the score-sheet.

The declarer? Bob Rowlands, arguably the best player in England during the last decade with no aspirations to play in international competition.

The final deal arose during the final session of the Polish trials of 1964.

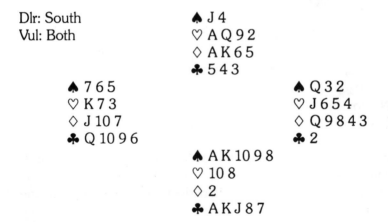

Dlr: South
Vul: Both

♠ J 4
♡ A Q 9 2
◇ A K 6 5
♣ 5 4 3

♠ 7 6 5
♡ K 7 3
◇ J 10 7
♣ Q 10 9 6

♠ Q 3 2
♡ J 6 5 4
◇ Q 9 8 4 3
♣ 2

♠ A K 10 9 8
♡ 10 8
◇ 2
♣ A K J 8 7

At this stage, there were only four tables in play. One pair reached seven clubs, going two down undoubled; the second North-South pair played in and made six notrump (perhaps by taking three major-suit finesses); and the third pair stopped in five clubs. But at the table under our spotlight, Aleksander Rozecki, partnered by Jerzy Wisniewski, was in six clubs, greedily doubled by West.

The opening lead was the jack of diamonds. Declarer took

dummy's two diamond winners, discarding a spade from hand, and ruffed a diamond. The queen of hearts was finessed successfully, the ace of hearts cashed, and a heart ruffed in hand. The ace-king of spades and ace of clubs were followed by a spade ruff in the dummy. Declarer was down to the king-jack of clubs and a spade, and West had three trumps remaining. Rozecki led a heart from the dummy and discarded his spade. West was compelled to ruff his partner's jack of hearts and lead into declarer's trump tenace.

West swore never to double a slam again. He realized, of course, that if he had not doubled, the slam would have failed, declarer playing on trumps.

Rozecki and Wisniewski represented Poland in the World Team Olympiad in New York in May of that year.

My Tip for a Top

When you feel the opponents have stepped out of line and you have a trump stack, think twice before doubling for penalties. Consider the caliber of the declarer and your risk. Unless you are sure of defeating this contract *and* any other they might attempt instead — preferably by at least two tricks — don't double, it may boomerang on you.

Don't give away your hand — leave the advertising to Madison Avenue!

Chapter 2

Direct the Opening Lead During the Auction

For all sad words of tongue or pen,
The saddest are these: "It might have been!"

Maud Muller, *Barbara Frietchie*

The fate of many contracts hinges upon the opening lead. Strolling through the playing areas at a major bridge tournament, you pick up fragments of conversations, such as: "If only you had led a ..." or "Sorry, partner, I made the wrong lead, but ..." or "How could I tell that a ... lead would beat the contract?"

You see avid bridge players gathering around experts holding court. They cling to scraps of paper covered with bridge hands, eagerly awaiting their turn to ask: "Nobody vulnerable, the bidding was ... and you are on lead. Which card do you pick?"

The need to justify and rationalize one's actions is desperate, the egos of bridge players being sky-high.

Yet, did you ever examine your conscience after a catastrophic lead by your partner? Did you ever wonder whether some of the blame was yours, not all his? Had you done your best to steer him away from the lurking perils and guide him onto the road to success?

Here is an example which will eloquently illustrate the point I am trying to make. It occurred during the immensely popular Swiss Teams at the 1988 Fall Nationals in Nashville, Tennessee.

Sitting East with North-South vulnerable, I held

♠ K J 10 6 4 2 ♡ 4 3 2 ◇ A Q 2 ♣ 5

The bidding proceeded like this:

West	North	East	South
		2♠	3♡
4♠	4NT (a)	?	

(a) Roman Key Card Blackwood

Reflecting upon the nature of North's bidding, I decided that if RHO were good enough to use Blackwood, he must possess heart support and first- or second-round controls in all side suits. This seemed to mark North with the king of diamonds, so I introduced the lead-directing bid of five diamonds, hoping to score two diamond tricks.

South elected, maybe erroneously, to bid five spades, showing two key cards and the queen of trumps in their methods. This resulted in a final contract of six hearts.

My partner obliged by leading the four of diamonds, and these were the four hands:

```
Dlr: East              ♠ 9
Vul: N-S               ♡ K 9 8 6
                       ◇ K 10 9
                       ♣ A Q J 8 7
      ♠ Q 7 5 3                         ♠ K J 10 6 4 2
      ♡ 5                               ♡ 4 3 2
      ◇ 6 5 4 3                         ◇ A Q 2
      ♣ 10 9 4 3                        ♣ 5
                       ♠ A 8
                       ♡ A Q J 10 7
                       ◇ J 8 7
                       ♣ K 6 2
```

Grateful for partner's lead, I cashed two diamond tricks for one down.

At the other table, the bidding was less imaginative:

West	North	East	South
		2♠	3♡
4♠	4NT	5♠	6♡
Pass	Pass	Pass	

In the absence of other information, the opening lead was the three of spades, and our team-mates scored their vulnerable slam, two losing diamonds being discarded on dummy's clubs. Plus 1430 gave us a swing of seventeen imps.

The moral of this story can be summed up in:

My Tip for a Top

Instead of complaining about bad luck or your partner's leads, be aware of the opportunities to put in a lead-directing overcall in order to steer partner onto the right road needed for a successful defense.

You will be amazed how your scores will improve, and your partnership confidence will soar to imposing levels.

Direct the opening lead during the auction.

Chapter 3

Bid More with Six-Four

Shakespeare never had six lines together without a fault. Perhaps you may find seven, but this does not refute my general assertion.

Samuel Johnson

O ne of the areas of bidding often neglected by players is the correct evaluation of the usefulness of different hand patterns.

Of course, everyone has learned to prefer a shiny 5-5-3-0 distribution to the dull 4-3-3-3, but not much further thought is given to the fascinating subject of intrinsic playing values corresponding to various distributions.

Advanced players familiar with Jean-René Vernes' Law of Total Tricks will benefit from their knowledge in competitive auctions. They develop an awareness of the importance of trump fit, the increased value of a double fit, and the critical factor of distribution. The rule of thumb suggested by the Law of Total Tricks is that if the high-card strength is more or less evenly divided, each side can bid with relative safety for as many tricks as the number of trumps they each hold.

In this era of point-counters, few students of the game are acquainted with the Losing Trick Count (LTC) of F. Dudley Courtenay. Yet this method of hand evaluation reflects with astonishing accuracy the playing values of different hand patterns when a fit exists.

Using Courtenay's method in its simplified form, we count a loser for each missing ace, king or queen in any suit of three or more cards. In a doubleton suit, a missing ace or king is a loser. A singleton is a loser unless it is the ace. A void is counted for no loser.

In Romex, we have been using this method, together with the Cover Card concept developed by the author, with great success.

Assuming for a moment that a hand does not contain any ace, king or queen, we come up with the following table for the most frequent distributions:

Distribution	Losers	Frequency (%)
4-3-3-3	12	10.54
4-4-3-2	11	21.55
5-3-3-2	11	15.52
5-4-3-1	10	12.93
5-4-2-2	10	10.58
6-3-2-2	10	5.64
6-3-3-1	10	3.45
4-4-4-1	10	2.99
6-4-2-1	9	4.70
5-5-2-1	9	3.17
7-3-2-1	9	1.88
6-4-3-0	9	1.33
5-4-4-0	9	1.24
5-5-3-0	9	0.90
6-5-1-1	8	0.71
6-5-2-0	8	0.65

Let us disregard the remaining 2.22% of distributions, noting only that hand patterns with seven intrinsic losers are rare freaks.

Enough said about numbers and theory — back to real life!

At the 1989 Bermuda Regional — incidentally, a wonderful tournament characterized by the splendid hospitality of the organizers and the breathtaking beauty of the island — a number of fascinating 6-4 hands came up. They represented a good test for the proposed theory that if a trump fit is found, an opening bid with this pattern needs very little help from partner to make a game. (Alternatively, a good save is often possible against the opponents' game.) In each of the following, the power of the 6-4 distribution becomes evident.

The first three hands occurred during a pair event.

Dlr: South
Vul: Both

```
                      ♠ 10 9 7 2
                      ♡ 9 4 3 2
                      ◇ J 9
                      ♣ A Q 10
  ♠ Q 5 4                            ♠ A K 8 3
  ♡ Q 8                              ♡ 7
  ◇ K 10 7 5                         ◇ 8 6 2
  ♣ 8 7 6 4                          ♣ K J 9 5 3
                      ♠ J 6
                      ♡ A K J 10 6 5
                      ◇ A Q 4 3
                      ♣ 2
```

West	North	East	South
	Rosenkranz		Wold
			1♡
Pass	2♡	Dble	4♡
Pass	Pass	Pass	

In spite of only 22 combined points (seven of which were unneeded with the trumps splitting 2-1), Eddie Wold and I reached the excellent game.

Note that the top cards in the red suits convert the nine-loser 6-4-2-1 pattern to a four-plus-loser hand. The North hand has two cover cards (the ace of clubs is one, and the queen of clubs and doubleton diamond are half each), giving two-plus remaining losers.

Finally, observe that, with a good guess in the trump suit, East-West can get out for 500 in five clubs doubled, but who would ever find the sacrifice?

Dlr: South   ♠ 5
Vul: Both   ♡ 8 3
                       ◇ J 10 9 8 7 4
                       ♣ A J 7 3

♠ K Q 10 8 6   ♠ J 7 4 2
♡ A Q J   ♡ K 10 9 7 6
◇ Q 6   ◇ —
♣ 9 6 4   ♣ Q 10 8 5

                       ♠ A 9 3
                       ♡ 5 4 2
                       ◇ A K 5 3 2
                       ♣ K 2

West	North	East	South
	Rosenkranz		Wold
			1 ◇
1 ♠	2 ◇	4 ♠	Pass
Pass	5 ◇	Pass	Pass
Pass			

What would you bid over one spade with that North hand? It is the sort of problem that is used for bidding panel articles in the bridge magazines. Let us look at the possibilities.

Two diamonds is an underbid.

Three diamonds, if a limit raise, is feasible. If you use three diamonds as a preemptive raise, you could cue-bid with two spades.

A preemptive three diamonds is an underbid too.

Three or four clubs, if played as fit-showing, are reasonable, but would normally show four diamonds and six clubs.

Four diamonds is reasonable too. Partner might wish to double four spades; and if he goes on to five diamonds, your hand will not be a disappointment. The drawback is that four diamonds carries you past three notrump. This brings us to a key factor. What does your one-notrump opening show? If you are using the strong notrump, there is less reason to worry about three notrump being your only game. Playing the weak notrump, there is more reason to consider that contract. We, of course, were using the Romex notrump, so my partner could have had a weak or strong notrump!

Five diamonds looks excessive, even with the 6-4 shape. It could easily be a phantom sacrifice.

As there seemed to be no "right" answer, I chose to go slowly, bidding only two diamonds. There was bound to be more bidding, and I hoped to be able to judge better on the next round.

When East's four spades came back to me, I had to go on with five diamonds. I just hoped it was not a phantom sacrifice; and if it were not, it rated to be a good save — or a good make!

As you can see, five diamonds was laydown. We could have beaten four spades if we had found our club ruff, but that would have been little consolation for a missed vulnerable game.

Dlr: East
Vul: Both

```
                    ♠ Q 9 7 3
                    ♡ 8 5 2
                    ◇ J 8 7 6
                    ♣ A 3
    ♠ 8                           ♠ A 4
    ♡ J 9 4                       ♡ K 10 7 6 3
    ◇ K 10 9 3 2                  ◇ A Q 5
    ♣ J 10 8 7                    ♣ K Q 5
                    ♠ K J 10 6 5 2
                    ♡ A Q
                    ◇ 4
                    ♣ 9 6 4 2
```

West	North	East	South
	Wold		Rosenkranz
		1♡	1♠
2♡	2♠	3♡	3♠
Pass	Pass	4♡	4♠
Pass	Pass	Pass	

In spite of holding only ten high-card points, I was tempted by my 6-4 shape and the favorable heart position to bid four spades directly over East's cautious three hearts. Surely West would lead a heart even if he had the king. In a team game, I would have bid four spades, not giving the opponents two bites at the cherry. In a pair event, though, bidding thin games usually does not pay. It was possible three spades would be passed out. However, when East went on with four hearts, I bid the game.

Four spades made easily — and East did well not to double. This time, our combined count was only seventeen points (of which two were unnecessary). As with the previous deal, we can defeat four hearts if we organize a club ruff — but it would still be small recompense for a vulnerable game. Also, if you transfer the king of hearts to the West hand, they make their game and four spades is either a good save or a make, depending upon the opening lead.

Finally, this little gem. It was the first board from the last round of the Swiss team event between two of the quartets vying for victory.

```
Dlr: South              ♠ 8 4
Vul: Both               ♡ A Q 8 2
                        ◇ J
                        ♣ A K 10 9 6 5
        ♠ A Q 7 6 3 2                   ♠ K 10 9 5
        ♡ 7                             ♡ 3
        ◇ K 10 9 6 2                    ◇ A Q 4 3
        ♣ Q                             ♣ J 8 7 3
                        ♠ J
                        ♡ K J 10 9 6 5 4
                        ◇ 8 7 5
                        ♣ 4 2
```

West	North	East	South
	Wold		Rosenkranz
			3♡
3♠	4♡	4♠	Pass
Pass	5♡	Pass	Pass
5♠	6♡	Dble	Pass
Pass	Pass		

Wold, encouraged by his gigantic 6-4, bid his hand skillfully, suppressing his powerful club suit. Also, he was afraid that if he jumped directly to six hearts, he would stampede the opponents into six spades. The penalty from that contract rated to be less than the value of a vulnerable game — and at worst would be no penalty at all!

The limit for both sides was eleven tricks, so six hearts was a good sacrifice. However, as Wold never bid the suit, West decided to lead his singleton queen of clubs. (In the cold light of day, this is the wrong lead, especially with only a singleton trump. But it is much easier to say that when you can see all 52 cards.) Making the slam was now routine, and we chalked up an unusual plus 1660.

The good news was that in the other room our opponents played in five hearts, and we won fourteen imps. The bad news was that we lost the match and the event on the last board.

My Tip for a Top

I hope these examples have convinced you that my argument is sound. Next time you pick up a 6-4, bear these things in mind:

In competitive situations, pay close attention to your hand pattern.

Try to visualize your partner's distribution.

With 6-4: bid more!

Chapter 4

Competing for Partscores at Imps

Thou shalt not covet; but tradition
Approves all forms of competition.

The Latest Decalogue, *Arthur Hugh Clough*

With a perfect record of 7-0, you are playing the last match for the championship of a National Swiss Team event against the only other undefeated team. With a good-looking scorecard and no errors, you confidently return for the comparison to your home table. Your expectations are deflated when you find that in the last hand where, after a spirited auction, your opponents made an innocent looking three-diamond partscore for minus 110 points, your team-mates sold out to two spades for minus 110. The fatal double partscore swing of six imps again reared its ugly head and caused you to lose the coveted event.

This common scenario repeats itself innumerable times at imp scoring, and only a relatively small number of players know the basic components of correct decision making. At matchpoints the problem is even more complex, and the competition for partscores is subject to more factors, many depending on the caliber and psychology of your opponents.

Therefore let us focus on imp scoring and look at the following two basic situations, assuming always that the high-card strength is more or less evenly divided between the competing sides.

1. No eight-card or longer fit exists

The limit of the hand is generally one notrump; any bid at the two-level will result in a minus score.

Advice: Compete at the one-level, but sell out at the two-level and try to get a plus score.

2. The opponents have found an eight-card or better fit

Very likely your side also has an eight-card or better fit. The Law of Total Tricks by the great French theorist Jean-René Vernes gives you an excellent guideline to determine your level of safety and how high to compete.

I won't go into detail describing his findings, but I will give you a simple rule of thumb which will tell you how high to compete when the high-card strength is more or less equally divided between the two opposing sides:

> Compete to the two-level with a eight-card fit
> to the three-level with a nine-card fit
> to the four-level with a ten-card fit

In other words, *bid for as many tricks as your side has trumps*. This rule is very reliable; however, it can be relaxed slightly when you have a double fit (see example hand two below).

Other important considerations in competitive situations are:

1. Location of high cards. Is your strength concentrated in your suit(s) or do you have values in their suit(s)? In other words, are your values offensive or defensive? Are you missing any trump honors?

2. How is the opponents' trump suit splitting? A two-card holding in their suit is generally the worst (partner may have two or even three cards). One or three cards is an improvement; a void or (rarely) four cards excellent.

3. If you have the master, or higher-ranking, suit and can bid at the same level without having to go higher, you have an advantage.

4. With very distributional hands and a double fit, bid one more.

5. If you have a slight edge in the balance of high cards, be more conservative and protect your plus score. A small plus is better than going minus.

6. Be very careful competing at the four-level; the opponents have the choice of doubling you or bidding on.

7. If having considered all this you are still in doubt, bid one more. Who knows, you may make your contract or the opponents may take the push.

Here are two examples from a Swiss Team event provided by Ron

Andersen. The first illustrates the principle of going plus.

Dlr: South	♠ J 9 3 2		
Vul: Both	♡ K 10 7 5		
	◊ Q 9 4		
	♣ K 7		

♠ 7		♠ K Q 8 6 4	
♡ Q 6 3		♡ 8	
◊ K J 10 3		◊ A 8 7 5	
♣ A 10 9 6 2		♣ 8 4 3	

♠ A 10 5	
♡ A J 9 4 2	
◊ 6 2	
♣ Q J 5	

West	North	East	South
			1♡
Pass	2♡	Pass (a)	Pass
2NT (b)	Dble (c)	3◊	Pass (d)
Pass	Pass (e)		

(a) Short of the values to enter the auction directly over two hearts; partner is "listening" to the bidding should the auction die at two hearts.

(b) Even vulnerable playing imps, West should not sell out to two hearts; the opponents have established a fit, increasing the likelihood that West's side has a fit. Passing could easily result in a double partscore swing.

(c) Showing a maximum single raise; inviting partner to act with this knowledge.

(d) Nothing more to say, leaving the decision up to partner.

(e) At matchpoints, North should either double or bid three hearts. At imps, pass is clear.

In the end, declarer lost one spade, one heart, one diamond and two clubs to finish one down: minus 100. A flat board against minus 110 in two hearts, but on a good day East would have guessed how to make three diamonds.

The second hand illustrates the value of the double fit.

Dlr: South   ♠ A 10 9 8
Vul: None   ♡ 7 4 2
                    ◇ K 10 9 5
                    ♣ 8 6

♠ J 5		♠ 7 6 2
♡ A 10 5 3		♡ K Q J 6
◇ J 4		◇ 8 6 3
♣ A 9 7 4 3		♣ K J 10

                    ♠ K Q 4 3
                    ♡ 9 8
                    ◇ A Q 7 2
                    ♣ Q 5 2

West	*North*	*East*	*South*
			1◇
Pass	1♠	Pass	2♠
Pass	Pass	Dble	Pass
3♣	3◇	Pass	3♠
Pass	Pass	Pass	

The double fit, in spite of only two eight-card fits, enables North-South to score plus 140 while East-West can win nine tricks with either rounded suit as trumps by guessing the queen of clubs.

My Tip for Top:

When competing for partscore at imps, after both sides have found a fit and hold about half of the high cards: Protect your plus score; don't bid to go minus.

Chapter 5

Interference over Two Clubs

"My aunt was suddenly prevented from going on a voyage in a ship that went down — would you call that a case of Providential interference?"

"Can't tell; didn't know your aunt."

Archbishop William Temple

You pick up a beautiful hand and open two clubs, strong, artificial and forcing. You are looking forward to a slow, easy-paced auction to the perfect contract. All your hours of work are finally going to pay off when you and your partner score an undisputed top. But suddenly there is a spanner thrown into the works: one of the opponents has the temerity to overcall.

What is your immediate reaction? To double, to try to teach him a lesson? To shuffle uncomfortably in your chair, wishing you and your partner had spent just one minute discussing this possibility?

True, the opponents will not overcall that often, but it pays to sort out your countermeasures. First of all, let us look at matters from the point of view of the responder. The traditional approach has been for the responder to bid a respectable suit with positive or near-positive values, to pass with any hand that has no convenient bid (which is forcing, of course), and to double with a bad hand containing length and strength in the overcaller's suit.

For example, your partner opens two clubs and the next player bids two hearts. What would you bid with each of these hands?

a. ♠ K J 10 7 6 5   b. ♠ K Q 8 3   c. ♠ 4
   ♡ 3   ♡ 5 4 2   ♡ Q J 9 6 5
   ◇ Q J 3   ◇ Q 6 3   ◇ 9 8 4 3
   ♣ 7 6 3   ♣ Q 4 3   ♣ 7 6 2

Using these traditional methods, you bid two spades with hand *a*; make a forcing pass with *b*; and double with *c*. Hand *a* is a little thin for a normal positive response, but you should show your suit. If you pass and your left-hand opponent raises the ante, it might be impossible to get across a good description of this hand.

Having said that, there are two other schools of thought. One group uses the double in the negative sense, showing a scattering of values. Hand *b* above would be an ideal example. They pass with any really bad hand *or* a penalty double of the overcall. This has two advantages. The first is the similarity to the handling of overcalls at the one-level. And it allows a "penalty" double when the responder makes a negative double and finds the opener at home with a good, long holding in the overcaller's suit.

The drawback, always a risk with negative doubles, is that the opener might not believe his partner can have a penalty double, so he doesn't balance with a double, instead bidding his own suit.

The second camp uses the double like a double negative to show a very bad hand. It tells the opener that he is on his own. A pass promises either some points, being equivalent to a negative double, or is a penalty double of the overcall; a bid shows a good suit with positive values; and a cue-bid guarantees a strong hand.

Employing this style, you would bid two spades with hand *a*; pass with hand *b*; and, strange as it may seem, with *c* you pass also, hoping partner balances with a double.

Discuss these possibilities with your partner and decide which approach you prefer.

Now let us move to the other side of the table. The opener has started the proceedings with two clubs, the responder has bid a waiting (or negative) two diamonds, and now an opponent comes into the auction. What are the meanings of the opener's various rebids?

Here, I think, experts are as unanimous as experts are ever likely to be. The opener bids his primary suit if he has an unbalanced hand. But with a balanced hand that was planning to rebid in notrump, he passes with an unimpressive holding in the overcaller's suit, or doubles with a long and strong holding in the overcaller's suit: a holding with which he wants the responder to pass almost regardless of his hand. He is saying that he feels confident the penalty will outscore any game and probably any small slam. Only if the responder is strong and distributional should he consider removing the double.

Here is an example from the Stratified Pairs at the 1991 Spring Nationals in Atlantic City.

Dlr: South   ♠ 10 6
Vul: E-W   ♡ Q 10 5 3
                              ◇ Q 9 8 3
                              ♣ 8 5 2

♠ A K Q 9   ♠ J 7 5 4 2
♡ K 4   ♡ J 9 8 7 6 2
◇ A J 10 7   ◇ K
♣ A Q 4   ♣ 3

                              ♠ 8 3
                              ♡ A
                              ◇ 6 5 4 2
                              ♣ K J 10 9 7 6

A lot of Souths opened three clubs, trading on the vulnerability. But at one table, this was the auction:

West	North	East	South
			Pass
2♣	Pass	2◇	3♣
Dble	Pass	Pass	Pass

The double is an error. That hand doesn't mind playing in three clubs doubled, but it shouldn't insist. It is right to pass. If the responder has a relatively balanced hand too, he will double and then the opener can pass. Here, of course, the responder will cue-bid with four clubs and six spades should be bid fairly easily.

True, the double could have outscored all pairs playing only in game. West led a top spade and, after seeing the dummy, decided to play his partner for the king of diamonds. Given that decision, it is correct to switch to the *seven* of diamonds. East wins with the king and returns a spade. West wins, cashes the ace of diamonds, and leads the jack of diamonds, East ruffing away dummy's queen.

In this way, the defenders collect two spades, three diamonds, one diamond ruff and two clubs for plus 800.

At the time, West switched to the ten of diamonds, showing zero or two higher honors, declarer played low from the dummy and 800 was impossible.

My Tip for a Top

Once you have discussed the common situations with your partner, try to cover the irregular, especially those that will swing a lot of points like the auctions following interference after a two-club opening.

If you have opened two clubs with a balanced hand, only double an overcall by your RHO when you want partner pass almost regardless of his hand.

Chapter 6

Bidding Over 1M-(Double)

A taste for drink, combined with gout,
Had doubled him up for ever.

The Gondoliers, *W.S. Gilbert*

Several methods have been proposed and successfully introduced following these two starts to an auction: 1♡-(Dble)-? and 1♠-(Dble)-?

The most recent contribution is *Cappelletti Over One of a Major Doubled* (C/1MX).

Our Romex group have adopted this excellent approach, but we have added our own slight modifications. Here are the general principles:

1. All bids by the responder from one notrump to two of the suit *under* the opener's major suit, inclusive, are *transfers*. But as the responder did not redouble, they indicate fewer than eleven points. (1♡-[Dble]-1♠ is natural and forcing.)

2. The transfer into a new suit usually indicates length, but may be made for lead-directing purposes when also holding the values for a good single raise of the opener's major. But the transfer should never be employed with fewer than three cards in the "shown" suit.

3. The transfer into opener's major shows a good three- or four-card raise.[1] The exact nature is clarified on the next round.

4. The bid of two of opener's suit is the weakest raise, equivalent to the uncontested auction of 1M-1NT-2X-2M, the responder holding three-card support for the major but only 6-7 points.

---

[1] From the Law of Total Tricks, normally you will restrict this transfer bid only to a *three*-card raise. A *four*-card raise usually should get the bidding immediately to the three-level (or higher). However, if you have the sterile 4-3-3-3 distribution with four trumps, you might judge the hand is not worth a raise to the three-level. Then you would make this transfer bid.

5. New suits at the three-level (and two spades over one heart) are preemptive. (Alternatively, they can be played as fit-showing.)

6. New suits at the four-level (and three spades over one heart) are splinter bids promising at least four-card support for the opener's major. (Alternatively, they can be played as fit-showing.)

7. The redouble shows more than ten points, but denies four-card or longer trump support.

8. Two notrump is "Truscott", promising a balanced limit raise with at least four-card support and one-and-a-half defensive tricks *outside* the trump suit.

9. Three of opener's major is preemptive (normally with four trumps).

10. Three notrump is a game-force with at least four-card support.

11. Four of opener's major is preemptive (normally with four trumps and a void or five-plus trumps).

12. Finally, what do you do with a "normal" one-notrump bid: 7-9 points with no side suit to show and only two-card support for partner? We recommend that first you pass, then you double or raise partner's major to the two-level!

Further Developments

Opener accepts the transfer only if he would have passed a non-forcing natural bid in that suit by the responder. Otherwise he makes his normal rebid. (We play that the opener cannot pass the transfer because the responder could have three-card support for his major.)

For example:

West	North	East	South
	1♡	Dble	2♣
Pass	2◇		

North would have passed a non-forcing two-diamond response.

West	North	East	South
	1♡	Dble	1NT
Pass	2◇		

North would not have passed a non-forcing two-club response. Instead, he prefers to play in either red suit.

There are two bids that require special attention.

If the responder shows an immediate raise by transferring into the opener's major, and then bids a new suit after opener repeats his suit, it is a mini-splinter.

For example:

West	North	East	South
	1♠	Dble	2♡
Pass	2♠	Pass	3◇

South shows spade support with two hearts, and a singleton diamond with three diamonds.

If the responder continues with two notrump after transferring into the opener's major, it shows a balanced 10-11 points with three-card trump support.

If the responder makes a transfer into another suit and the opener bids into that suit, the responder may continue by showing a single or jump three-card major-suit raise, or bid a new suit as a natural game-try.

Interference by the Doubler's Partner

If the responder makes a transfer bid into a new suit and the doubler's partner (often called the advancer) bids a new suit at the two-level, *double* by the opener promises tolerance for the suit shown by the responder. It is similar to a fit-showing double, and asks the responder to describe his hand further.

If the advancer bids at the three-level, a double is more penalty-oriented.

Example Hands

As always, the best way to illustrate a bidding method is by showing a few examples. The auction has begun 1 ♡ -(Dble)-? What would you bid with each of these hands?

a. ♠ Q J 10
♡ 7 3
◇ K 10 8 4
♣ J 10 4 3

b. ♠ Q J 10 9
♡ 7 3
◇ K 10 8
♣ J 10 4 3

c. ♠ 7 5
♡ J 7 3
◇ K 10 8 4
♣ J 10 4 3

d. ♠ K Q 3
♡ J 5 2
◇ Q 6 5 2
♣ Q 10 9

e. ♠ 7 5
♡ Q J 10
◇ K J 7 4
♣ K J 7 4

f. ♠ J 5 3 2
♡ K J 9
◇ 8
♣ K J 5 4 2

g. ♠ Q J 4
♡ Q J 10
◇ K 9 8
♣ J 10 9 2

h. ♠ 7 4
♡ K Q 10 3
◇ Q 8 7 3
♣ J 10 9

i. ♠ K 4
♡ Q J 10 3
◇ A 10 7 3
♣ 8 5 3

j. ♠ K Q 3
♡ J 7 4
◇ K 8 4 3
♣ K 10 3

k. ♠ 3
♡ K J 7 4 2
◇ J 8 3
♣ K 10 7 2

l. ♠ 3
♡ K J 7 4 2
◇ A J 8 3
♣ K 10 7

m. ♠ K 5
♡ Q 10 7 2
◇ A J 3
♣ K 7 6 2

n. ♠ J 5 4
♡ 7
◇ K J 10 9 7 4
♣ Q 5 4

o. ♠ J 5 4
♡ 7
◇ Q 5 4
♣ K J 10 9 7 4

p. ♠ 7 5
♡ 10 8 6
◇ A K J
♣ 10 7 5 3 2

q. ♠ 7 5
♡ Q 10 8
◇ A K J
♣ 10 7 5 3 2

r. ♠ K 5
♡ Q J 8 7 5
◇ A K J 10 8
♣ 4

s. ♠ K 9 7 6
♡ A J 9
◇ 4 3
♣ A Q 6 5

t. ♠ 6 5
♡ 7 2
◇ K J 10 8
♣ A Q 7 5 4

u. ♠ 6 5
♡ Q 8 7 5
◇ K Q 7 5 4
♣ A 5

Here are my suggested answers:

a. Pass. Double or bid two hearts (or pass) at your next turn.

b. 1♠. Make your natural bid.

c. 2♡. A bad single raise, with only one-and-a-half cover cards.

d. 2♢. A transfer into partner's major. You plan to follow up with two notrump, showing 10-11 points, a three-card raise and a notrump-type hand.

e. 2♢. As above, but bid three hearts on the next round to show a good balanced three-card raise that is less suitable for notrump.

f. 2♢. Transfer into hearts, intending to bid three diamonds to show a mini-splinter with three-card support.

It is dangerous to try this sequence with four-card support because the extra trump is so valuable. It is worth about a king, and there is a risk the opener will misjudge.

g. 2♢. As in d; the hand is not strong enough for any other action.

h. 3♡. A preemptive raise with four trumps. Unless you use a conventional bid like three clubs to show a good single raise with four trumps, often this will be bid with a single raise not good enough for "Truscott."

i. 2NT. Truscott. A limit raise with four-card support and one-and-a-half defensive tricks outside hearts.

j. Redouble. Twelve high-card points, only three trumps and practically all one's values outside the trump suit: a "book" bid.

k. 4♡. A good preemptive raise to game, very little defense, five trumps and a singleton in the other major.

l. 3♠. An ace stronger than the previous hand, making it strong enough for an immediate splinter bid.

m. 3NT. A balanced game-force with four-card support and no interest in extracting a low-level penalty.

n. 2♣. A transfer to diamonds, intending to pass if partner rebids two diamonds. If playing preemptive jumps, bid three diamonds.

o. 1NT. The same hand as above, but with the minors transposed. However, bid three clubs if using preemptive jump shifts.

p. 2♣. A diamond lead-directing bid, but you intend to correct to hearts later.

q. 2♣. The same hand as above, but with one more cover card. You will follow up with a value bid in partner's major.

Note that if the responder holds a fourth trump:

♠ 7 5 ♡ Q 10 9 8 ◇ A K J ♣ 10 5 3 2

he would like to start with two clubs, pinpointing the diamond lead, but it is too dangerous. Suppose the advancer jumps to three spades. The opener will have to assume the responder holds a diamond one-suiter, and if he passes, the responder will be forced to bid four hearts to show his support. And what if the advancer jumps to *four* spades? Now it is even worse. The responder will have to double, but never to show the four-card heart support is frightening. You should bid two notrump, Truscott, and hope that if they outbid you in spades, your partner doesn't blow a trick with a heart lead.

r. 4NT. Not wasting any time, you explore for slam with Roman Key Card Blackwood.

s. Redouble. You will jump in hearts on the next round, showing a good three-card raise with thirteen-plus points.

t. 1NT. A transfer to clubs. You plan to continue with two diamonds on the next round.

u. 3 ◇. Playing fit-showing jump shifts, this shows four-card trump support and a good five-card side suit. If the jump is preemptive, your bid is two notrump. Don't redouble with four-card support.

My Tip for a Top

To improve your methods when the opponents double your major-suit opening bid, give the above methods a try. I'm sure your results will improve.

Chapter 7

What Does it Mean when You Double an Opponent's Cue-Bid?

The billiard sharp whom any one catches,
His doom's extremely hard —
He's made to dwell —
In a dungeon cell
On a spot that's always barred.
And there he plays extravagant matches
In fitless finger-stalls
On a cloth untrue
With a twisted cue
And elliptical billiard balls.

The Mikado, *W.S. Gilbert*

How often does it occur that, in the course of a competitive auction, an opponent cue-bids your suit? Almost instinctively, you reach for the red "D" card if you are using bidding boxes, or, in less Olympian settings, you vocally express your opinion of this action by quietly, or loudly, doubling.

This double may mean:

a. I take this as a personal insult.
b. I urge you to lead my suit, partner.
c. We may have a good "save" here.
d. Lead something else!

The first of these is a luxury no bridge player can afford.

Unless partner has a very good lead of his own, he'll probably lead your suit anyway. But, because he *might not* do so, my partners and I have agreed to have the second interpretation for the double.

The third possibility is less likely, but with luck it will be apparent when you wish to apply this meaning to the double. Probably you would have made a preemptive bid earlier in the auction.

The last possibility is becoming more popular among experts. Reason *d* is a Lightner-type double, and it must be alerted. The argument is that there is little point in doubling just to hear your own voice as it gives your left-hand opponent the choice of passing, redoubling or making an informative free bid, gratefully accepting this extra opportunity your double has provided. Also, partner rates to lead your suit, so only by doubling can you get him to lead another suit. However, if you do wish to use interpretation *d* for the double, handle with care. Make sure your partner understands it, otherwise you are looking at a bleak future!

An eloquent example of not doubling "just because" came up while we were playing against a famous British pair in the 1986 Olympiad in Miami. This was board nine from the Open Pairs:

Dlr: West
Vul: N-S

```
                    ♠ J 10 6 5
                    ♡ K 10 5 2
                    ◇ K 2
                    ♣ A 9 2
    ♠ 9 3                           ♠ A Q
    ♡ 7 4                           ♡ Q J 8 6 3
    ◇ A 10 7 4 3                    ◇ Q 9 8 5
    ♣ J 10 7 6                      ♣ Q 3
                    ♠ K 8 7 4 2
                    ♡ A 9
                    ◇ J 6
                    ♣ K 8 5 4
```

West	North	East	South
Reygadas	Teltscher	Rosenkranz	Rose
Pass	Pass	1♡	1♠
Pass	2♡ (a)	Pass (b)	2♠
Pass	Pass	Pass	

(a) Limit raise in spades
(b) Not particularly interested in a heart lead

Partially quoting from the Daily Bulletin: "Miguel Reygadas took note of his partner's pass of two hearts, so he made the testing lead of the three of diamonds from his ace. Not surprisingly, the British champion, Irving Rose, guessed wrongly and George Rosenkranz won with the queen of diamonds. Looking ahead, George correctly diagnosed that the only future lay in the club suit; he therefore returned the queen of clubs and Miguel encouraged with the six (an upside-down attitude signal). Dummy won with the ace of clubs. Next came the jack of spades, and East rose with the ace of spades to fire back the three of clubs. This went to the king, and now declarer led the jack of diamonds, hoping to get some useful information about the trump suit. To Irving's dismay, Miguel took the ace of diamonds, cashed a high club and played a fourth club. Dummy ruffed this, but Rosenkranz overruffed with the queen of spades. This razzle-dazzle defense provided the Mexican pair with 125 out of 138 matchpoints."

This hand points up the value of having a firm understanding of what a double of a low-level cue-bid means. Defense can be a beautiful artistic experience, but it takes two to tango!

There is some icing you can apply to the cake. If you do double the cue-bid to demand the lead of your suit, the attitude and probably also the count will be known. Thus you can indicate suit preference practically at trick one through the size of the card you play in your suit.

The following deal includes this suit preference signal.

Dlr: East
Vul: None

		♠ A 6 5 2	
		♡ J 10 7 4	
		◇ K 7 3	
		♣ K 7	
♠ 9 4			♠ K Q J 10 7
♡ K 8			♡ 5 2
◇ 9 6 5 4 2			◇ A Q J
♣ 9 6 4 2			♣ 8 5 3
		♠ 8 3	
		♡ A Q 9 6 3	
		◇ 10 8	
		♣ A Q J 10	

West	North	East	South
		1♠	2♡
Pass	2♠ (a)	Dble (b)	4♡
Pass	Pass	Pass	

(a) Limit raise in hearts
(b) "Please, lead my suit!"

West obediently led the nine of spades, and declarer won in dummy with the ace. East played the king of spades to this trick as a suit preference signal asking for dummy's higher-ranking side suit: diamonds. Without this agreement, it would have been more difficult for West to choose his return after the trump finesse lost to his king of hearts. At this point, spades, diamonds and clubs are all possible returns, but only a diamond shift defeats the contract.

My Tip for a Top

When the opportunity of doubling RHO's cue-bid presents itself: think twice. Only if you are absolutely sure you want the lead of the cue-bid suit, insist with the double.

Chapter 8

A Different Lead-Directing Double

So double was his pains, so double be his praise.

The Faerie Queen, *Edmund Spenser*

One of the "musts" of an active bridge writer and competitor is to keep up with the literature. I myself derive considerable pleasure and intellectual stimulation from this activity which others may consider a chore.

Reading Terence Reese's and David Bird's interesting book, *The Hidden Side of Bridge*, I was gratified to witness that the authors quoted and commented upon a hand from my *Modern Ideas in Bidding* in connection with the double of splinter bids. In this book, in 1982, together with Alan Truscott, I recommended a different use for the double of a splinter bid than just to convey the natural meaning, namely, length and strength in that suit. The reasons for this proposal were weighty:

1. In contrast to doubles of cue-bids or relays, the double is not needed to request the lead of the splinter suit, because the lead of dummy's short suit will more often than not give away a trick or a tempo.

2. With favorable vulnerability, sometimes the splinter bid can be brushed aside, to bid the suit as a sacrifice.

3. Much more valuable for the defense is the double of the splinter bid to suggest the lead of a specific suit.

In this respect one can detect a certain similarity to the "Lightner Double" which says: "Don't lead this suit but..." I have employed this idea with substantial success in many different partnerships, independently of the system played.

The following agreement sums it up:

A. If a splinter bid is doubled and two unbid suits remain, the double calls for the lead of the lower-ranking of the two unbid suits.

B. With only one unbid suit remaining, the double requests the lead of that suit.

The pass, of course, carries the corresponding negative inference. Thus, in *A*, the pass expresses doubt or a preference for the higher-ranking unbid suit. In *B*, the pass says: "You are on your own."

Not a bad idea for letting you exercise your gray cells.[1]

To illustrate the advantages of this approach, two hands spring to mind. The first was from the 1985 Mexican Trials. Both sides are vulnerable and you are sitting West, holding

♠ Q J 10 3   ♡ 2   ◇ J 10 9 7 5   ♣ J 6 2

The bidding proceeds:

West	North	East	South
			1♡
Pass	4◇	Dble	4♡
Pass	Pass	Pass	

Without the double you would have led the queen of spades, or maybe the jack of diamonds, but here partner has requested a club lead. You finger the two of clubs when it occurs to you that this may not be sufficient because you may never regain the lead to push a second club through. Confident in your analysis, you lay the *jack* of clubs onto the table.

These were the four hands:

---

[1] How about a double of a Blackwood four-notrump bid in an uncontested auction? I suggest that it is lead-directing for the *lowest* logical suit. This is the one you are least likely to be able to double later in the auction.

Dlr: South   ♠ A 8 4 2
Vul: Both   ♡ A J 8 7
                               ◇ 8
                               ♣ K 9 7 4

♠ Q J 10 3   ♠ 9 6 5
♡ 2   ♡ Q 10 3
◇ J 10 9 7 5   ◇ 6 4 3 2
♣ J 6 2   ♣ A Q 10

                               ♠ K 7
                               ♡ K 9 6 5 4
                               ◇ A K Q
                               ♣ 8 5 3

As you can see, the jack of clubs is the only lead to beat the contract.
On any other lead declarer can discard two losing clubs from dummy
on his diamond honors.

The mandated lead produces four tricks for your side, three
clubs and a heart, thanks to the conventional lead-directing double.

Eddie Wold furnished me with this little gem from one of the
countless Regional tournaments in his busy schedule. Sitting West
with only the opponents vulnerable, he held

♠ Q J 10 7 4   ♡ A 9   ◇ 8 7 3   ♣ 9 7 4

The auction progressed like this:

West	North	East	South
	1♣	Pass	1♡
Pass	3♠	Dble	Pass
Pass	4♡	Pass	Pass
Pass			

Under normal circumstances one would lead a spade, or maybe the
ace of hearts to take a look at the dummy. But partner's double
rings like an alarm clock: "Please lead the unbid suit." Obediently,
Wold led the three of diamonds and, to his delight, these were the
four hands:

Dlr: North
Vul: N-S

```
                    ♠ 8
                    ♡ K Q 6 5
                    ◇ K J 4
                    ♣ A K 10 5 3
♠ Q J 10 7 4                          ♠ 9 6 5 3 2
♡ A 9                                 ♡ 4 3
◇ 8 7 3                               ◇ A Q 10 5
♣ 9 7 4                               ♣ 8 6
                    ♠ A K
                    ♡ J 10 8 7 2
                    ◇ 9 6 2
                    ♣ Q J 2
```

North played the jack of diamonds and East won with the queen. This was an excellent start, but *per se* not fully sufficient. To his credit, East worked out the only return to set the contract: a trump. Of course, West rose with ace and led back the eight of diamonds to seal the fate of the contract.

I hope these examples convince you to give my idea a try, so here is:

My Tip for a Top

Use the double of an opponent's splinter bid as a lead director.

When two suits have been named, the double requests the lead of the lower-ranking unbid suit.

When three suits have been bid, double for the lead of the fourth suit.

In all other situations, your pass tells your partner to work it out for himself, using his own judgment.

Chapter 9

Red for Danger

Out of this nettle, danger, we pluck this flower, safety.

Henry IV, Part 1, *William Shakespeare*

Alan Truscott is the source of one of my favorite bridge stories. A bridge teacher gives to four of his students a slip of paper with the following hand written on it:

♠ — ♡ A K 9 8 5 4 ◇ 9 7 3 ♣ A 10 9 5

The teacher says, "You are in fourth seat and the bidding goes one spade-pass-four spades to you."

Turning to the first pupil, he asks, "What is your bid?"

"Double," says the first student.

"Wrong! Next."

"Five hearts," comes the fast answer.

"Wrong again."

"I know: four notrump," counters the third student.

"Absurd," growls the annoyed professor.

"Pass," comes the triumphant last reply.

"You all failed to find the right answer," announces the teacher.

"Impossible," the students chant in unison.

"Not at all. None of you asked what the vulnerability was, so you are all wrong!"

That is the essence of this article. Apart from the well-known Rule of Two and Three for preempts, guidelines for sacrifices, a warning to be careful when vulnerable, and to avoid the fatal minus 200 number at matchpoints, the information you can find in textbooks is scant.

Yet, all experts recognize the importance of the vulnerability in the bidding, and making the necessary adjustments has become second nature to them.

For example, Kaplan and Kay are playing "Timid K-S" with a weak notrump not vulnerable and a strong notrump when vulnerable. Goldman and Soloway go to the extreme of playing two different systems: a strong club method non-vulnerable and Scientific Standard when vulnerable. But the average player seldom reflects upon the dynamic changes he should make to his bidding methods as the vulnerability varies.

Our main Romex nucleus, Eddie Wold, Miguel Reygadas and myself, have also followed this path. At imps, when the vulnerability is favorable we use a mini notrump (10-12 points), and a strong club with Romex-style responses. At matchpoints, we use this system whenever we are non-vulnerable. At other times, we stick to classic Romex.

"Why is that so?" you may ask. The answer is that competitive bidding is a complex subject, and bridge writers tend to avoid topics which are difficult to explain, especially when space is limited.

Nor do I intend to delve too deeply. I would rather present you with a smorgasbord of selected examples to whet your appetite, and to encourage you to be increasingly aware of the numerous situations which arise during the bidding. They occur more often than you may realize.

Take a hand like this one:

♠ K Q 10 9 4 ♡ Q J 7 ◇ 6 4 2 ♣ 8 6

Your right-hand opponent opens one club. Not vulnerable, there is little risk involved in overcalling one spade (some players would even jump preemptively to two spades), and a lot to gain. The overcall will serve as a lead-directing bid, perhaps stopping the opponents from playing in three notrump, and may even suggest a possible sacrifice. Also, it pays to hold spades. You force the opponents to go to the next level to outbid you. With equal vulnerability, the overcall becomes more risky; and red against white it is downright foolhardy.

Here is another situation. After two passes, you are looking at

♠ 8 5 3 ♡ K Q J 10 ◇ Q 8 6 5 ♣ J 9

With favorable vulnerability, a one-heart opening would be the choice of most experts, and, with both sides non-vulnerable, a few would still take the same action. But when the red color appears in the board, an overwhelming majority would pass.

Responding to partner's overcalls varies considerably under different vulnerability conditions. Interestingly enough, you should be more willing to compete with a fitting hand after partner's vulnerable overcall than after a non-vulnerable one. Take this South hand from a matchpoint duplicate:

♠ Q 9 8 ♡ 6 3 ◇ 10 9 8 7 4 ♣ A 4 2

With North-South vulnerable and the dealer West, the bidding began (1♣)-1♠-(3♣). Under the stated conditions, South should raise to three spades. With both sides non-vulnerable, the raise becomes more debatable as North may have a weakish hand and the opponents may elect to take their penalty instead of contracting for a dubious game.

On this occasion, North held

♠ K J 10 3 2 ♡ Q 7 4 ◇ A K Q 3 ♣ 3

and the vulnerable game was duly reached after South's three-spade bid. Ten tricks were there for the taking thanks to the double fit, the opponents being unable to organize a diamond ruff.

Here is another competitive situation. Sitting South, you are the dealer, holding

♠ K J 10 6 5 ♡ J 4 ◇ A 7 5 ♣ K Q 3

The bidding starts:

West	North	East	South
			1♠
2♡	2♠	3♡	?

Not vulnerable, you should compete with three spades, but vulnerable a pass is the right choice. The opponents may make eight, nine or ten tricks, depending on the lie of the cards in the black suits, but you are a favorite to lose five tricks. Vulnerable, the danger of minus 200, the "kiss of death," is too great.

When the bidding comes around to you in fourth seat after an opening bid and two passes, and you have length in the opener's suit, the vulnerability can play a decisive role. Suppose you hold:

♠ K 9 8 ♡ K Q J 9 ◇ Q J 9 ♣ A 10 3

When LHO's one-heart opening is passed round to you, pass is the right choice if the opponents are vulnerable. You hope for the magic plus 200 number (or better). But against non-vulnerable opponents, a reopening bid of one notrump (or perhaps a less desirable double) is advisable, as you may chalk up a score that exceeds plus 100.

At imp scoring, the relative vulnerabilities have an additional significance. I am sure you are aware that when playing matchpoints you strive for a plus score because it is the frequency of wins that matters, and therefore you tend to be more conservative in border-line situations. However, at imps the amount of the gain is crucial. A vulnerable game should be bid with as little as a 37 percent chance of success.

Here is an example. In first position, you open one club with

♠ K 9 5 ♡ 10 4 ◇ A J 8 ♣ K J 10 9 6

In an uncontested auction, your partner responds one heart, you rebid one notrump, and he makes an invitational raise to two notrump. Not vulnerable, you will pass conservatively; but vulnerable at imps you should try three notrump.

Partner's hand was

♠ Q 10 3 2 ♡ A 9 5 3 ◇ 10 3 ♣ A 7 2

On a diamond lead and a successful guess in clubs, nine tricks were duly made.

Let us return to the hand introduced at the beginning of this article:

♠ — ♡ A K 9 8 5 4 ◇ 9 7 3 ♣ A 10 9 5

With equal or favorable vulnerability, you should take action and bid five hearts, but when vulnerable against not, the pass is more prudent.

I hope the foregoing examples have made you aware of the bidding problems caused by the various vulnerabilities.

To end:

My Tip for a Top

When you have to make a decision whether to enter the auction or to remain silent, keep a watchful eye on the vulnerability. Your action should be dictated by not only your vulnerability but also that of your opponents.

Before making any move, weigh the possible gain against the risk involved.

Section B

Defense

The Prologue

Courtship to marriage, as a very witty prologue to a very dull Play.

The Old Bachelor, *William Congreve*

1. You are seated in the West chair and both sides are vulnerable. Your hand is:

♠ 9 8 2　♡ 9 6 3　♢ K J 6 2　♣ K J 4

The auction proceeds like this:

West	North	East	South
			1♢
Pass	1♠	Pass	2NT
Pass	3NT	Pass	Pass
Pass			

What is your opening lead?

(Page 66)

2. Dlr: East
Vul: Both

♠ K 10 7 5 3
♡ 5 3
♢ 10 8 5
♣ A 7 3

♠ A Q 9 6 2
♡ 7
♢ A 7 6 3
♣ K 5 4

West	North	East	South
		4♡	4♠
Pass	Pass	Pass	

West leads the jack of hearts, East overtaking with the ace and returning the nine of hearts. You ruff with the ace of spades, West following with the four. Do you see any way to avoid three minor-suit losers?

(Page 74)

3. Dlr: North   ♠ Q J 4 3
Vul: E-W   ♡ A K Q 5
                                 ◇ A Q 6 2
                                 ♣ Q
   ♠ K
   ♡ 10 9 6
   ◇ 8 7
   ♣ A J 10 7 6 5 3
   West   *North*   *East*   *South*
                   1◇   Pass   1♠
   2♣   4♣ (a)   Pass   4♠
   Pass   Pass   Pass
(a) Splinter bid

You lead the ace of clubs: queen, four, king. What do you lead at
trick two?

(Page 85)

4. Dlr: East   ♠ A 7
Vul: Both   ♡ A Q J 10 6 3
                                 ◇ Q 7 4
                                 ♣ Q 2
                                                 ♠ K Q
                                                 ♡ 7 4
                                                 ◇ K J 3
                                                 ♣ A K J 8 5 4
   West   *North*   *East*   *South*
                                    1♣   2♠
   Pass   3♡   4♣   Pass
   Pass   4♠   Pass   Pass
   Pass

West leads the six of clubs: two, jack, nine. You cash the king of
clubs: three, seven, queen. What do you lead at trick three?

(Page 86)

5. Dlr: South ♠ 8 3
Vul: E-W ♡ K J 10 9
◇ Q 10 9 4
♣ Q 10 4

                                    ♠ A J 9
                                    ♡ 7 5 2
                                    ◇ 7 6 2
                                    ♣ 9 8 7 3

West	North	East	South
			1♣
Pass	1◇	Pass	1NT (a)
Pass	2NT	Pass	3NT
Pass	Pass	Pass	

(a) 15-17 points

West leads the two of spades, fourth best. When dummy plays low, which card do you table?

Assuming you play the ace, declarer drops the five. How do you continue?

(Page 92)

6. Dlr: South ♠ A K Q 4
Vul: Both ♡ Q 10 7
◇ 7 6 5
♣ 8 4 2

                                    ♠ J 10 5
                                    ♡ A J 9
                                    ◇ Q J 8 3 2
                                    ♣ Q 10

West	North	East	South
			1NT
Pass	2♣	Pass	2◇
Pass	3NT	Pass	Pass
Pass			

West leads the ten of diamonds. Declarer wins with the king and starts to run dummy's spades. Do you see any chance to defeat the contract?

(Page 112)

7. Dlr: East   ♠ A 9 7 2
Vul: N-S   ♡ Q 10
                                ◇ A Q
                                ♣ K 7 6 5 2
                                                        ♠ K 6
                                                        ♡ A K 7 4
                                                        ◇ 10 9 6 2
                                                        ♣ 10 9 8

West	North	East	South
		Pass	1♠
Pass	3♣	Pass	3◇
Pass	3♠	Pass	4♣
Pass	4◇	Pass	4♡
Pass	4♠	Pass	6♠
Pass	Pass	Pass	

West leads the six of hearts. Plan the defense.

(Page 113)

8. Dlr: South   ♠ 9 8 6 3 2
Vul: None   ♡ J 2
                                ◇ A K Q
                                ♣ 8 4 3
                                                        ♠ Q J 10
                                                        ♡ A Q 3
                                                        ◇ 7 6 5 3 2
                                                        ♣ 9 2

West	North	East	South
			1♠
Dble	2NT (a)	3◇	4♠
Pass	Pass	Dble	Pass
Pass	Pass		

(a) Spade fit, defensive values

West leads of the jack of diamonds, declarer taking dummy's three winners, discarding the six and seven of hearts. South continues with three rounds of trumps, West pitching two low hearts and his last diamond. What is your best chance to defeat the contract?

(Page 125)

9. Dlr: South   ♠ J 5
Vul: None   ♡ 10 2
                   ♦ A K 3
                   ♣ A K 9 7 5 4

                             ♠ A 4
                             ♡ Q J 9 3
                             ♦ Q 8 7 6
                             ♣ J 6 3

West	North	East	South
			2♠
Pass	2NT	Pass	3♡ (a)
Pass	4♠	Pass	Pass
Pass			

(a) Maximum weak two-bid with a heart feature

The opening lead is the ten of clubs. Declarer wins in his hand with the queen and leads the six of spades to the jack, West playing the three. How do you defend?

(Page 130)

10. Dlr: North   ♠ K 7 4
Vul: Both   ♡ A
                   ♦ A Q 8 5 3
                   ♣ K Q 8 2

                               ♠ A J 10
                             ♡ 9 5 3
                             ♦ K J 7
                             ♣ J 9 6 3

South plays in four hearts, having shown a weak hand with long hearts. Wests leads a low spade, declarer putting up dummy's king. After winning with the ace, what do you lead next?

(Page 144)

11. Dlr: North   ♠ A K
Vul: None   ♡ A K 9 8 7
                                  ◇ Q J 7 5
                                  ♣ J 5

        ♠ Q 8 6 3
        ♡ J 10
        ◇ A 8 6 4 3
        ♣ A Q

West	North	East	South
	1♡	Pass	Pass
Dble	Redble	1♠	2♣
2♠	3♣ (a)	3♠	4♣
Pass	Pass	Pass	

(a) Sporting!

You lead the three of spades. Declarer wins in the dummy, cashes the ace-king of hearts, and continues with the nine of hearts. Your partner plays the queen, declarer ruffs with the nine of clubs, and you overruff with the queen.

How do you continue from here?

If you cash the ace of diamonds, it is covered by the five, two and nine.

(Page 134)

12. Dlr: North   ♠ K Q 10 6 3
Vul: Both   ♡ 9 7 6
                  ◇ A 7 6
                  ♣ A 6

                           ♠ J 9 4 2
                           ♡ J 8 4 2
                           ◇ 8 5 4
                           ♣ K 8

West	North	East	South
			1NT
Pass	2♡ (a)	Pass	2♠
Pass	3NT	Pass	4♠
Pass	Pass	Pass	

(a) Transfer bid

West leads the jack of diamonds, denying a higher honor. Declarer wins with dummy's ace and plays four rounds of spades, losing the last to your jack. West discards in order the four, seven and three of clubs, and declarer pitches the five of hearts.

Now you switch to the four of hearts, playing third- and fifth-highest leads, declarer winning with the ace and West dropping the three. Next, South runs the queen of clubs to your king.

This is the six-card end-position you are surveying:

                 ♠ 10
                 ♡ 9 7
                 ◇ 7 6
                 ♣ A

                         ♠ —
                         ♡ J 8 2
                         ◇ 8 5
                         ♣ 8

What do you lead at trick eight?

(Page 132)

Chapter 1

You Can't Remember What You Don't See!

The best way to suppose what may come, is to remember what is past.

George Savile, Marquis of Halifax

This chapter could be subtitled *A Tale of the Honeybee, the Miser and the Solo Artist*.

Bridge players often complain about having bad memories, using this as an excuse for their mistakes. My standard reply to this popular lament is: Few people are born with bad memories; lack of concentration and poor habits of observation are the real culprits. What you don't see cannot be remembered!

I must admit, however, that there are some mechanical problems to overcome if you want to be a keen observer. The change in the laws about the examination of current and quitted tricks has a lot to do with it. Contrary to previous practice, nowadays if you have turned your card face down on the table, you lose your right to examine the cards played to that trick. So beware and don't prematurely flip over the card you have just played: leave it face up. Otherwise your all-important chance to have a good look at the trick is gone.

Losing track of earlier tricks occurs frequently after a long, tiring session, and may become very costly.

However, there is a good reason not to remember a card: When it has never been played.

It is surprising how often average defenders forget the cards, particularly in high-level contracts. Conceivably their lack of high cards dampens the interest of one or both defenders, and the need to convey vital information about the distribution is not recognized.

Excluding top notch defenders, there are three prototypes I like to call the Honeybee, the Miser and the Solo Artist.

The first group seems disinterested in the happenings around the table, or maybe believes in not telling the enemy or partner anything. When it comes to discarding, he stumbles from one suit to another, seemingly without purpose — like the Honeybee savoring the nectar of various colorful flowers.

Here is an example:

Dlr: South   ♠ Q 10 7 5 2
Vul: Both   ♡ J 8 6 5
          ◇ J 9 4
          ♣ 5

```
        ♠ 8 6                          ♠ K J 9 4 3
        ♡ 9 4 3 2                      ♡ Q 10 7
        ◇ 8 7 6 2                      ◇ Q 5 3
        ♣ 9 8 6                        ♣ 4 2
```

         ♠ A
         ♡ A K
         ◇ A K 10
         ♣ A K Q J 10 7 3

West	North	East	South
			2♣
Pass	2◇	Pass	3♣
Pass	3♠	Pass	7NT
Pass	Pass	Pass	

South won the opening lead of the nine of clubs in his hand and proceeded to play all his clubs but one, on which West discarded a spade, a heart and a diamond. But look at poor East's problem at trick six. This was the position:

         ♠ Q 10
         ♡ J 8 6
         ◇ J 9
         ♣ —

```
     ♠ 8                              ♠ K J
     ♡ 9 4 3                          ♡ Q 10 7
     ◇ 8 7 6                          ◇ Q 5 3
     ♣ —                              ♣ —
```

         ♠ A
         ♡ A K
         ◇ A K 10
         ♣ 3

What could East discard? With no help from partner, he guessed to throw the three of diamonds. Curtains!

An attentive and experienced West would discard in this order: eight of spades, six of spades, four of hearts. East would know it was safe to abandon all his spades as there is no entry to dummy. When declarer plays his last club at trick seven, West completes his echo in hearts and a grateful East stubbornly conserves his diamonds to defeat the contract.

Let us observe the antics of the Miser during the following hand. His weakness manifests itself in holding onto a useless card which could never take a trick, thus misleading partner.

```
Dlr: South              ♠ 5 3
Vul: Both               ♡ 8 7 6 4
                        ◇ J 6 5 4
                        ♣ Q 7 6
        ♠ 9 8 2                         ♠ 10
        ♡ 10 3 2                        ♡ A J 9 5
        ◇ 10 7 3                        ◇ Q 8 2
        ♣ K 8 4 3                       ♣ J 10 9 5 2
                        ♠ A K Q J 7 6 4
                        ♡ K Q
                        ◇ A K 9
                        ♣ A
```

West	North		East	South
				2♣
Pass	2◇		Pass	2♠
Pass	3♣	(a)	Pass	6♠
Pass	Pass		Pass	

(a) Second negative

The opening spade lead was won by declarer, who drew two more rounds of trumps, on which East discarded the jack of clubs and five of hearts. South played the king of hearts, West signaled with the two, and East won with the ace. His return was the ten of clubs, won with declarer's ace while West signaled with the eight.

South's next plays were three more rounds of trumps and the queen of hearts, which resulted in this four-card ending:

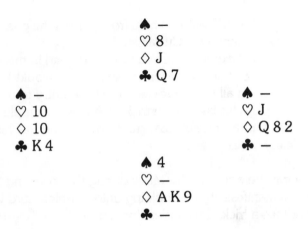

When declarer led his last trump the Miser discarded the four of clubs, clinging desperately to the ten of hearts while dummy pitched the eight of hearts. East was convinced that declarer still held the ten of hearts. Reluctantly he parted with the two of diamonds, with fatal results. Notice that had the Miser discarded his useless ten of hearts, East could let go of his jack of hearts and defeat the slam.

The last example shows the Solo Artist. Characteristically, he is concerned only with his own holding, discarding his idle cards without even trying to help partner in the defense. He doesn't believe in giving count and haughtily ignores informative discards.

Dlr: South   ♠ 8 6 4
Vul: N-S   ♡ A K 7
                     ◇ K J 2
                     ♣ 9 7 6 5

♠ 9 2		♠ J 10 7 3
♡ J 9 6 3		♡ Q 10 8 2
◇ 8 7 5 4 3		◇ 9 6
♣ 3 2		♣ Q J 10

                     ♠ A K Q 5
                     ♡ 5 4
                     ◇ A Q 10
                     ♣ A K 8 4

West	North	East	South
			2♣
Pass	2◇ (a)	Pass	2NT (b)
Pass	4NT	Pass	6NT
Pass	Pass	Pass	

(a) Waiting
(b) 22-23 points

The Solo Artist led the eight of diamonds, won with dummy's jack. Declarer played a club to the king, and ducked a club. South won the diamond return with the ace and cashed his two top clubs. West discarded two useless diamonds and East threw the two of hearts.

However, when the king of diamonds was played East had a problem. This was the position:

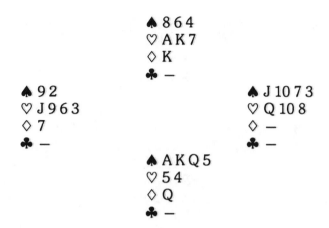

He made the wrong guess and discarded the three of spades, allowing South to score his slam.

What went wrong? Had West discarded his two useless spades on the third and fourth rounds of clubs, East would have protected the spade suit and parted with the eight of hearts, thus foiling the pseudo-squeeze.

My Tip for a Top

Observe carefully and keep track of the cards played when defending.

Don't get bored with bad hands.

Help partner by giving count when he badly needs the information.

Unless it will help the declarer, throw all the cards from a suit you do not intend to protect before making a discard in another suit.

Chapter 2

Unblocking on the Opening Lead

Not merely a chip of the old 'block', but the old block itself.

On Pitt's First Speech, *Edmund Burke*

Often I have written about unblocking plays; but here is yet another possibility. A spectacular application occurs occasionally when choosing the opening lead against an opponent's three-notrump contract.

You can recognize this situation from the following characteristic features:

1. Most of the outstanding high cards are usually in *your* hand.

2. You have no five-card or longer suit.

3. Partner has at most one entry.

In desperation, you try to hit partner's long suit, leading from a three-card holding including two untouching honors: for example, A J x, K J x or A 10 x.

However, it will not be enough to guess partner's long suit; you will have to lead the right card. In order to avoid blocking the suit, it is normally right to lead the *middle* card: a somewhat unusual approach.

Here are two examples from the 1989 Mexican Nationals.

Dlr: South   ♠ A J 7 6 3
Vul: Both   ♡ K J 10 4
                        ◇ 10 8 4
                        ♣ 5

♠ 9 8 2   ♠ 10 5 4
♡ 9 6 3   ♡ A 7 5 2
◇ K J 6 2   ◇ 3
♣ K J 4   ♣ Q 10 9 6 2

                        ♠ K Q
                        ♡ Q 8
                        ◇ A Q 9 7 5
                        ♣ A 8 7 3

West	North	East	South
			1◇
Pass	1♠	Pass	2NT
Pass	3NT	Pass	Pass
Pass			

Holding eight points himself, West knew that his partner probably held at most six points. He also had no attractive lead in sight, so he hoped his partner had some length in clubs and a side entry. West led the *jack* of clubs.[1]

Declarer ducked the ace of clubs until the third round, but East had to get in with the ace of hearts and the contract went one down.

In the other room, the contract was four spades by North. Even though East led his singleton diamond, ten tricks were safely gathered in. A swing of twelve imps to the good guys!

On the next deal, the Grand Lady of Mexican Bridge, Magda Sanchez Fogarty, made a brilliant play.

Magda was responsible for introducing tournament bridge in

---

[1] With specifically this holding, there is a case for leading the king. Perhaps it depends upon your leading agreements. If the king asks for an unblock, and your partner might not work out you must be short in the suit, maybe you had better start with the jack. However, if the jack promises no higher honor in the suit, starting with the king could work better.

Mexico during World War II, and organized the first duplicate contest for the benefit of the Red Cross. She was also a National Women's Doubles tennis champion during the '40s. In her spare time, she has been one of our leading bridge experts for over 50 years. Nowadays she plays less frequently, dedicating her time to her flowers; but the years have not affected her brilliance at the table.

Dlr: North
Vul: E-W

```
                    ♠ K J 7 2
                    ♡ 8 6
                    ◇ A K 9 2
                    ♣ 5 3 2
    ♠ A 10 3                       ♠ Q 8 6 5 4
    ♡ K J 10 7 4                   ♡ 9 5 3 2
    ◇ —                            ◇ Q 5 3
    ♣ K J 9 8 7                    ♣ 4
                    ♠ 9
                    ♡ A Q
                    ◇ J 10 8 7 6 4
                    ♣ A Q 10 6
```

West	North	East	South
	Pass	Pass	1◇
1♡	Dble (a)	Pass	1NT
2♣	3♣	Pass	3NT
Pass	Pass	Pass	

(a) Negative

Even given the prevailing vulnerability, East, Lolita Quezada (who represented Mexico in the 1991 Venice Cup playoff against Canada), was cautious in the bidding. However, if she had propelled her partnership into four hearts, probably it would have gone one down, and certainly it would have ruined a beautiful story.

The lead was the three of spades. The declarer, Miguel Reygadas, won with dummy's king and cashed the ace of diamonds. Seeing the endplay coming, West jettisoned the *ace* of spades!

Winning the third round of diamonds, East switched to the two of hearts. South rose with the ace, ran the diamonds, and exited with the queen of hearts in this end-position:

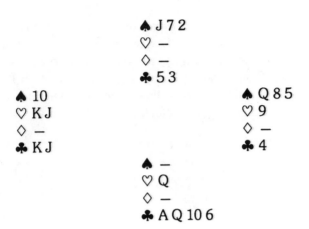

Magda cashed her second heart trick before leading the ten of spades. Declarer played low from the dummy, but East overtook and switched to her club. Brilliant defense for one down!

It is interesting to note that declarer has no chance on the opening lead of the *ten* of spades. This is more evidence for the validity of my argument.

My Tip for a Top

If the only chance to beat the opponent's (three-notrump) contract seems to be to lead from a three-card suit headed by two untouching honors, lead the middle card for an early unblock.

Chapter 3

A Switch in Time Saves Nine

A line will take us hours maybe;
Yet if it does not seem a moment's thought,
Our stitching and unstitching has been naught.

Adam's Curse, W.B. Yeats

The word "switch" has a familiar ring to railroad workers and electronics professionals. Yet, bridge players tend to forget this valuable maneuver in spite of the fact that the latest edition of the American Collegiate Dictionary includes among its definitions of the word: "A change to a suit other than the one played or bid previously."

My favorite, which I like to call the "Pendulum Defense," involves switching to a new suit after the opener's holdup at trick one; then, after a further holdup in the second suit, returning to the suit originally attacked.

Here is an instructive example from a team event in a Mexican Nationals.

Dlr: South
Vul: N-S

	♠ 10 9 6		
	♡ J 9 7		
	◇ J 10 6		
	♣ A Q J 4		

♠ Q J 8 4
♡ A 8 3
◇ 5 4
♣ 10 9 8 7

West	North	East	South
			1NT
Pass	2♣ (a)	Pass	2◇
Pass	2NT	Pass	3NT
Pass	Pass	Pass	

(a) Doesn't promise a four-card major if raising to two notrump

West led the two of hearts, fourth best. Dummy put in the nine and East won with the ace. What would you do now?

In a pair event, you would have a difficult decision. A spade switch would cost a vital overtrick if declarer holds something like

♠ A K 5   ♡ Q 6 5   ◇ K Q 9 8   ♣ K 3 2

But it was teams and East could tell that the heart suit couldn't supply enough tricks to defeat the contract. So, instead of automatically returning the eight of hearts, he switched to the four of spades, this being a better card than the queen in case declarer holds

♠ K 5   ♡ K 6 5   ◇ A K 9 8 7   ♣ K 3 2

Declarer did not try to block the suit by rising with the ace, so West won with the king and returned the suit, which declarer was forced to duck again. Now East went back to hearts, hoping to establish his partner's suit while he still had a diamond entry.

This was the full deal:

```
Dlr: South            ♠ 10 9 6
Vul: N-S              ♡ J 9 7
                      ◇ J 10 6
                      ♣ A Q J 4
    ♠ K 3 2                              ♠ Q J 8 4
    ♡ Q 10 4 2                           ♡ A 8 3
    ◇ K 3 2                              ◇ 5 4
    ♣ 6 5 3                              ♣ 10 9 8 7
                      ♠ A 7 5
                      ♡ K 6 5
                      ◇ A Q 9 8 7
                      ♣ K 2
```

Declarer won the fourth trick with the king of hearts, but when he took the diamond finesse, it lost and West cashed two more heart tricks to defeat the contract by two.

Notice that, against an immediate heart return, declarer makes nine tricks by rising with the king and conceding a trick to the king of diamonds. And it would not have helped declarer to win the second trick with the ace of spades as then the defenders would have scored three spades, one heart and a diamond.

Sharp-eyed readers will have spotted that an original spade lead will always beat three notrump, but that is almost impossible to find.

Here is another reason for switching; the hand comes from *Goren on Play and Defense*.

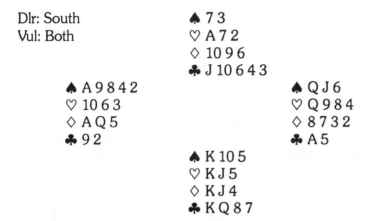

Dlr: South
Vul: Both

	♠ 7 3	
	♡ A 7 2	
	◇ 10 9 6	
	♣ J 10 6 4 3	

♠ A 9 8 4 2   ♠ Q J 6
♡ 10 6 3   ♡ Q 9 8 4
◇ A Q 5   ◇ 8 7 3 2
♣ 9 2   ♣ A 5

♠ K 10 5
♡ K J 5
◇ K J 4
♣ K Q 8 7

South opened and closed the auction with one notrump. West led the four of spades, South winning East's jack with the king. The declarer attacked clubs, East winning the second round. He cashed the queen of spades, West dropping the two to show that he had led from a five-card suit. At the same time East knew his partner had the ace of spades because with ♠ 10 9 8 4 2 he would have led the ten, not the four.

If East had played a third spade now, though, the contract would have made. But he realized that they needed two tricks from the red suits, and that diamonds looked more likely to come up with the goods than hearts. Also, as he wouldn't have the lead again, East decided he should switch to a diamond, selecting the eight to deny an honor. As you can see, this was the winning defense.

My Tip for a Top

Whenever the first suit you have led does not seem to promise sufficient tricks to defeat the contract, keep in mind the possible benefits of a switch to pastures new.

Chapter 4

Sluff the Aces, Keep the Deuces

To throw away the dearest thing he owed
As 'twere a careless trifle.

Macbeth, *William Shakespeare*

I am sure that when you read the title of this article a disapproving or incredulous frown will cross your countenance.

Of course, I am being slightly facetious, but there are times, albeit rare, when the foregoing statement is absolutely true.

To prove my point, I present two interesting hands. The first was played during a friendly match in 1970 between Great Britain and The Netherlands. It was held in Leiden, which lies between Amsterdam and The Hague. It features Jonathan Cansino, whose brilliant career was cut short by tragic illness, and Jeremy Flint, who died suddenly in November 1989.

```
Dlr: North              ♠ K 8
Vul: E-W                ♡ 9 5
                        ◇ Q J 10 8 6
                        ♣ Q J 9 6
        ♠ 6 5                           ♠ Q J 3 2
        ♡ 8 7 6                         ♡ K J
        ◇ 9 7 5 4 3                     ◇ A K
        ♣ A 5 2                         ♣ K 10 8 7 3
                        ♠ A 10 9 7 4
                        ♡ A Q 10 4 3 2
                        ◇ 2
                        ♣ 4
```

West	North	East	South
Cansino	Kokkes	Flint	Kreijns
	Pass	1♣	2♣ (a)
Pass	2◇	Pass	2♡
Pass	3NT	Pass	4♡
Pass	Pass	Pass	

(a) Michaels Cue-Bid showing a major two-suiter

Cansino found the best lead of a trump. Hans Kreijns — who won the World Open Pairs title in 1966 with Bobby Slavenburg — won the king with the ace and immediately took a spade ruff in the dummy, West parting with the two of clubs. The defenders seemed to be heading for three tricks only: one in each suit except hearts. However, it didn't work out like that.

A diamond was led from the dummy, and Flint won with the king. Next, he cashed the queen of spades *and West discarded the ace of clubs!* East continued with two rounds of clubs, promoting a trump trick to defeat the contract.

In the other room, West did not lead a trump against the same contract. Now declarer made his contract, and Great Britain gained ten imps.

It is a strange hand. In the room where a trump was not led, the defenders took a trump trick but the contract made. Where a trump was led, the defenders gained a side-suit trick and ended up getting the trump trick back with a promotion!

The story of the second hand comes from the late Walter Leipen, one of our great experts and the teacher of a whole generation of Mexican players. Born and raised in Vienna, he grew up with the famous school of Austrian pre-war experts. An accomplished technician, he was an ardent advocate — just like many of his world champion compatriots — of a club system, long before Italians and Americans turned to the countless forms of forcing club.

The following hand illustrates the brilliant card play and defense of these old-timers. Unfortunately, my notes don't tell me who the hero of my story was: Jellinek, Schneider, Stern, Frischauer or maybe another member of the 1937 World Championship team. The play is the hallmark of a true champion.

Dlr: East   ♠ K 10 7 5 3
Vul: Both   ♡ 5 3
                                 ◇ 10 8 5
                                 ♣ A 7 3

    ♠ J   ♠ 8 4
    ♡ J 4   ♡ A K Q 10 9 8 6 2
    ◇ K Q J 9 4   ◇ 2
    ♣ Q J 10 9 2   ♣ 8 6

                                 ♠ A Q 9 6 2
                                 ♡ 7
                                 ◇ A 7 6 3
                                 ♣ K 5 4

West	*North*	*East*	*South*
		4♡	4♠
Pass	Pass	Pass	

West's lead of the jack of hearts was overtaken by East's ace, and back came the nine of hearts. Declarer ruffed with the ace of spades, and cashed the queen of spades, dummy unblocking the seven and East the eight. The next three tricks were won with the ace of clubs, ace of diamonds and king of clubs in that order. Finally, South cast adrift by leading the two of spades and calling for dummy's three! East had to win the trick with the four and lead a heart. Declarer discarded a club from hand and a diamond from the dummy. On the next heart, declarer ruffed and West was squeezed.

My Tip for a Top

Occasionally you have to get rid of an ace, or the highest outstanding card, to avoid being thrown in. Keep the possibility in mind.

Also, it is a good idea to retain your lowest card in a suit if you can afford it — you may need it later for communication, or to endplay your opponent, or to avoid being endplayed yourself.

Chapter 5

Those Elusive Tricks: Take Them or Leave Them

Ah, take the Cash in hand and waive the Rest.

The Rubaiyat of Omar Khayyam, Edward Fitzgerald

One of the most frequent and tantalizing problems a defender faces is to decide when to cash out (taking his winning trick or tricks immediately) and when to wait.

At imp scoring this dilemma is less serious as the main objective is to defeat the contract. Overtricks, or even the additional undoubled undertrick, are generally less important: the emphasis is on safety.

At matchpointed pairs or board-a-match teams, however, the scenario is completely different. I found this out a very long time ago at a Houston Regional. I was playing with one of my Texan mentors, the great Benny Fain. Our vulnerable opponents stepped out of line, sacrificing against our non-vulnerable game and, of course, being doubled. They were rapidly one down and I could have cashed out for an additional undertrick. However, having visions of 800 and a glorious top, I waited and ... the tricks disappeared. Finally we had to settle for plus 200 and a miserable result. Fortunately we won the event and I became a Life Master, but I will never forget Benny's words: "If you see a good thing, take it; do not try for the best ... it may not arrive."

So the most important question you have to ask yourself when faced with a cash-out situation is this: Can the trick go away if I don't take it now? If the answer is in the affirmative, you are well advised to steer the conservative course and play out your winner(s). You may be surprised at the large number of matchpoints you will receive by adopting this policy.

Let us look at a few common situations:

1. You double a voluntarily bid contract: Take the setting trick(s). Do not speculate unless the opponents have sacrificed. In this latter case, though, analyze how the inflicted penalty matches up with your probable score as declarer.

2. Cash out if failing to do so may result in your being squeezed or endplayed, costing you a trick.

3. It is more difficult to visualize that partner's trick(s) may disappear. Make him cash out if you suspect declarer can get rid of his loser(s).

4. If you have a sure trick, probably in trumps, that your partner will not expect, make him take his trick.

5. Do not cash out if there is no way for declarer to make his contract. You may come to an extra trick as a result.

A few hands will serve to illustrate these points. The first comes from the 1985 Life Master Pairs, and was defended by the eventual winners, George Steiner and Darryl Pedersen.

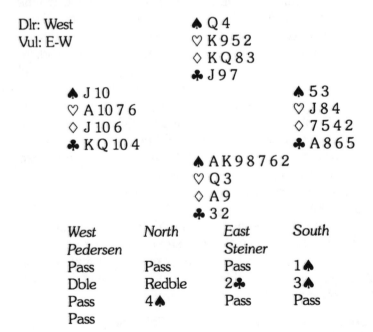

Dlr: West		♠ Q 4	
Vul: E-W		♡ K 9 5 2	
		◇ K Q 8 3	
		♣ J 9 7	

♠ J 10		♠ 5 3
♡ A 10 7 6		♡ J 8 4
◇ J 10 6		◇ 7 5 4 2
♣ K Q 10 4		♣ A 8 6 5

	♠ A K 9 8 7 6 2
	♡ Q 3
	◇ A 9
	♣ 3 2

West	North	East	South
Pedersen		*Steiner*	
Pass	Pass	Pass	1♠
Dble	Redble	2♣	3♠
Pass	4♠	Pass	Pass
Pass			

Pedersen led the king of clubs, and continued with the four when his partner encouraged. Noting his useless diamond spots, Steiner foresaw the possibility of heart discards, so he switched to a heart. Holding declarer to ten tricks was worth most of the matchpoints.

East had the opportunity to help his partner on the following deal from one of the European money tournaments.

Dlr: South	♠ 9 4 3 2		
Vul: E-W	♡ K 8 3		
	◇ A 4		
	♣ K Q 8 3		

♠ Q J 6	♠ 8
♡ 10 9 7 4 2	♡ A 6 5
◇ 7 6 2	◇ Q 9 5
♣ A 7	♣ J 10 9 5 4 2

♠ A K 10 7 5	
♡ Q J	
◇ K J 10 8 3	
♣ 6	

West	North	East	South
			1♠
Pass	3NT (a)	Pass	4♠
Pass	Pass	Pass	

(a) Balanced 12-15 points with four spades

West led the ten of hearts, East won with the ace and declarer dropped the queen. As South had to have the jack of hearts, it looked to East as though declarer was going to obtain a discard on dummy's king. As there was a risk that declarer had a low singleton club, East switched to the suit. West took his ace, and holding the declarer to ten tricks proved to be well above average for East-West.

This time you are sitting West at unfavorable vulnerability, holding

♠ J 9 3 2   ♡ A K 10 7 6 4 2   ◇ 10   ♣ A

The bidding proceeds:

West	North	East	South
	Pass	Pass	1♣
1♡	3♣	3♡	6♣
Pass	Pass	Pass	

What is your opening lead?

As he did not employ Blackwood, it is a virtual certainty that South has a heart void. As a consequence, you should get that ace of clubs out of your hand.

This was the full deal:

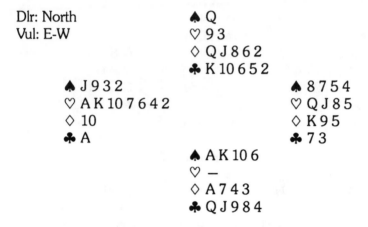

Dlr: North
Vul: E-W

```
                          ♠ Q
                          ♡ 9 3
                          ◇ Q J 8 6 2
                          ♣ K 10 6 5 2
      ♠ J 9 3 2                              ♠ 8 7 5 4
      ♡ A K 10 7 6 4 2                       ♡ Q J 8 5
      ◇ 10                                   ◇ K 9 5
      ♣ A                                    ♣ 7 3
                          ♠ A K 10 6
                          ♡ —
                          ◇ A 7 4 3
                          ♣ Q J 9 8 4
```

At the time, West led the king of hearts. Declarer ruffed, eliminated the majors, discarding two diamonds from the dummy, and finessed the queen of diamonds. When it held, he exited in trumps. Now he would make the contract if either the diamonds were 2-2 or the hand was as above, West being endplayed and forced to concede a ruff-and-sluff.

That hand was included in my *Trump Leads* book.

Finally, a deal I played in partnership with Lucho Konstantinovsky in Mexico City.

```
Dlr: North            ♠ K 10 3
Vul: N-S              ♡ K 10 2
                      ◇ K J 7 6
                      ♣ A 6 4
    ♠ Q                              ♠ J 9 6
    ♡ 9 7 5 4 3                      ♡ A 8 6
    ◇ A 4 3                          ◇ Q 10 9 8
    ♣ 10 9 8 7                       ♣ K 5 2
                      ♠ A 8 7 5 4 2
                      ♡ Q J
                      ◇ 5 2
                      ♣ Q J 3
```

West	North	East	South
	1◇	Pass	1♠
Pass	1NT	Pass	3♠
Pass	4♠	Pass	Pass
Pass			

My partner led the ten of clubs, and I won the first trick with the king. With nothing better to do, I returned the five of clubs, declarer winning with his queen. South led a low trump to the queen and king, and then tried the clever play of a low heart from the dummy. I rose with the ace and declarer dropped the queen. No doubt declarer was hoping in a moment to induce my partner to duck his ace of diamonds. Looking at three sure tricks, I did not want to lose the ace of diamonds if partner had it, so to thwart declarer's plan, I switched to the nine of diamonds. My partner took his ace and we were happy to defeat the contract.

My Tip for a Top

When faced with a cash-out situation, consider carefully whether or not a trick may go away. If there is a chance, either cash your winner or make partner take his. If the contract is unmakable, do not cash out; you may come to an extra trick later.

Chapter 6

Spot the Right Return

Three minutes' thought would suffice to find this out, but thought is irk-some and three minutes is a long time.

A.E. Housman

If you were to conduct a poll among bridge players, asking them to name their favorite part of bridge, bidding, declarer-play or defense, the choice by an overwhelming margin would be declarer-play. This is easily understandable as the declarer is on his own, but partnership cooperation is needed for the other two facets of the game.

Here is a problem relevant to the theme of this chapter:

Dlr: South	♠ Q 9 7		
Vul: Both	♡ Q 6 4		
	◇ K 2		
	♣ K J 10 8 7		

♠ 8 6 4 3 2
♡ A K J 10 3
◇ 8
♣ 3 2

West	North	East	South
			1 ◇
Pass	2 ♣	Pass	2 ◇
Pass	3 ◇	Pass	5 ◇
Pass	Pass	Pass	

West, your partner, leads the king of spades. Declarer wins with the ace and plays the queen of clubs from hand. West wins with the ace and switches to the five of hearts: four, ten and eight. What do you do now? (You use third-and-fifth-best, not fourth-best, leads.)

Defense is the most difficult part of bridge, especially for an occasional partnership. Often in the past I have stressed the need for detailed discussions on all aspects of the game, leading to a well-tuned, successful partnership. The problem above features a relatively frequent situation which, if left undiscussed, can produce disastrous misunderstandings at the table. The hand occurred in the Morning Knockout at the Lancaster Nationals in November 1989, which was won by the Rosenkranz team (Eddie Wold, Mike Passell, Mark Lair, Dan Morse and John Sutherlin). This was the full deal:

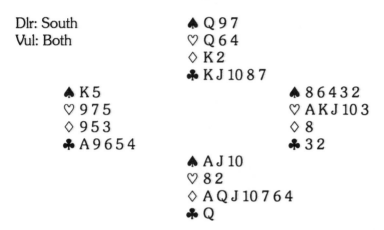

```
Dlr: South          ♠ Q 9 7
Vul: Both           ♡ Q 6 4
                    ◇ K 2
                    ♣ K J 10 8 7
       ♠ K 5                        ♠ 8 6 4 3 2
       ♡ 9 7 5                      ♡ A K J 10 3
       ◇ 9 5 3                      ◇ 8
       ♣ A 9 6 5 4                  ♣ 3 2
                    ♠ A J 10
                    ♡ 8 2
                    ◇ A Q J 10 7 6 4
                    ♣ Q
```

Against five diamonds, West led the king of spades, hoping to establish some quick winners before declarer could get discards on dummy's club suit. South won with the ace and played the queen of clubs from hand. West won with the ace and switched to the five of hearts, declarer dropping the eight. Thinking his partner had led a singleton spade, East tried to give his partner a ruff in the suit. Disaster! Declarer's second heart loser disappeared on the king of clubs and five diamonds made.

East was wrong for two reasons. When it is clearly a cash-out or give-a-ruff position, West should help his partner with a suit-preference lead. Wanting a spade ruff, West should return his highest heart, not his lowest. But there is a more telling reason. If declarer had a singleton heart, why wouldn't he be drawing trumps?

My Tip for a Top

To avoid misunderstandings, discuss in great detail your signaling methods with your regular partner.

Nevertheless, don't just blindly follow the signals — always *stop and think*.

Chapter 7

Who's Afraid of the Ruff-and-Sluff?

Trick'd in antique ruff and bonnet,
Ode, and elegy, and sonnet.

Anecdotes of Samuel Johnson, *Mrs. Piozzi*

One of the most serious problems facing bridge organizers at the moment is the increasing average age of the players. Fewer and fewer younger people are taking an interest in bridge, and college students, in contrast to the situation a decade ago, are finding the enticement of other pastimes like tennis, golf, computers — and even ten-pin bowling — more powerful than the lure of the pasteboards. Hopefully, good bridge software will rekindle the enthusiasm for the game among computer fans.

As a true *aficionado* and one who started to play bridge at the tender age of eleven, I seize every opportunity to find new talent, and encourage promising neophytes of our game. It was particularly gratifying one day when a young friend of ours dropped in for tea and was bubbling with excitement about bridge. He told us about his progress at the game, which he had taken up only the previous year. He was fascinated by the plethora of conventions, and spoke enthusiastically about the long list of rules he was learning: the do-and-do-nots of his teacher. As expected, ranking high in the order of priority was: "When defending, do not give a ruff-and-sluff to declarer." Certainly this is useful advice, but it is far from being one of the Seven Deadly Sins! Nor is it the big bad wolf of the children's song referred to in the title of this chapter.

At this stage of his bridge education, I did not want to disillusion my friend and undermine his confidence in his teacher. So I mumbled some encouraging words whilst at the same time thinking ahead to the time when he would be ready to learn that these aphorisms are not etched in imperviable stone. I thought of when I would be able to show him the following two hands. The first had occurred at our club in Mexico City. I am sure most of you will be familiar with the situation as it comes up quite often.

Dlr: North
Vul: Both

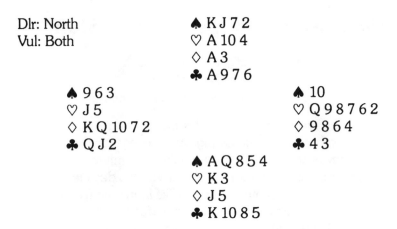

Against South's six-spade contract, West led the king of diamonds. Declarer won with dummy's ace, drew trumps, eliminated hearts, and threw West in with a diamond to give this five-card ending:

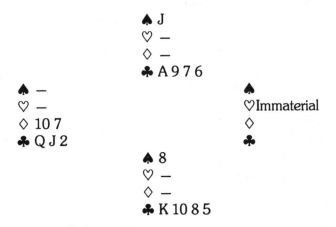

Mesmerized by the taboo about giving a ruff-and-sluff, West led a cagey jack of clubs. However, declarer guessed well, winning in hand with the king and running the ten through West to make his contract. Had West stopped to count, he would have realized that one club discard from either hand would do declarer no good. Then he would have led a diamond, conceding a ruff-and-sluff but defeating the slam.

My second hand is an antique, having been retained fondly among my notes for some 25 years. Playing with Margaret Wagar, one of the real greats of bridge and one of my all-time favorite partners, we were defending a title in the 1960 Mexican Nationals. This was the layout:

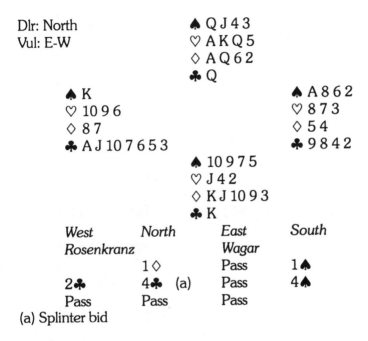

Dlr: North
Vul: E-W

♠ Q J 4 3
♡ A K Q 5
◇ A Q 6 2
♣ Q

♠ K
♡ 10 9 6
◇ 8 7
♣ A J 10 7 6 5 3

♠ A 8 6 2
♡ 8 7 3
◇ 5 4
♣ 9 8 4 2

♠ 10 9 7 5
♡ J 4 2
◇ K J 10 9 3
♣ K

West	North		East	South
Rosenkranz			Wagar	
	1◇		Pass	1♠
2♣	4♣	(a)	Pass	4♠
Pass	Pass		Pass	

(a) Splinter bid

I led the ace of clubs, and a look at the dummy convinced me that there was no point in a red-suit switch. The only hope was to take three tricks in the trump suit, so I played another club immediately, giving declarer a ruff-and-sluff and hopefully fatally weakening his trump holding.

Declarer ruffed in hand, discarding a diamond from the dummy, and played a trump to my singleton king. I continued with another club, and once more declarer pitched a diamond from the dummy and ruffed in hand. Next, he led his last trump, I threw a club and Margaret won with the ace before leading her final club. This was the straw that broke the declarer's back, and Margaret's fourth trump provided the setting trick.

Declarer could have tried an alternative line of play to give us a chance to go wrong — not that it would have helped him against Margaret! Instead of leading his last trump at trick five, declarer can cash two diamond and three heart tricks to give this position:

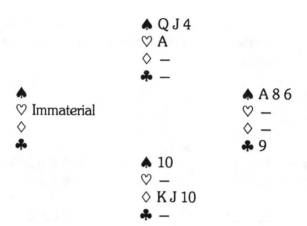

```
                          ♠ Q J 4
                          ♡ A
                          ◇ —
                          ♣ —
      ♠                                    ♠ A 8 6
      ♡ Immaterial                         ♡ —
      ◇                                     ◇ —
      ♣                                     ♣ 9
                          ♠ 10
                          ♡ —
                          ◇ K J 10
                          ♣ —
```

Dummy leads the ace of hearts and East has to ruff otherwise she takes only one trump trick. South overruffs and trumps a diamond high in the dummy, but East just discards her club to leave the dummy endplayed.

The last hand on this theme occurred during the 1987 Mexican Nationals.

Dlr: East   ♠ A 7
Vul: Both   ♡ A Q J 10 6 3
                              ◇ Q 7 4
                              ♣ Q 2

```
      ♠ 10 5 2                              ♠ K Q
      ♡ 9 8 2                               ♡ 7 4
      ◇ 9 8 6 2                             ◇ K J 3
      ♣ 10 7 6                              ♣ A K J 8 5 4
                              ♠ J 9 8 6 4 3
                              ♡ K 5
                              ◇ A 10 5
                              ♣ 9 3
```

West	North	East	South
Reygadas		*Rosenkranz*	
		1♣	2♠
Pass	3♡	4♣	Pass
Pass	4♠	Pass	Pass
Pass			

Clearly South should have bid four hearts at his second turn, but if he had, as the old line goes, there would have been no story.

Against four spades, my partner, Miguel Reygadas, led a club, and I won the first trick with the jack. Surely declarer had the ace of diamonds and, if he needed it, the heart finesse was working, so there was no future in either red suit. The only chance for a fourth defensive trick seemed to lie in the trump suit. As a consequence, I cashed the king of clubs and continued with the ace. Declarer ruffed in the dummy, discarded a diamond from hand, cashed the ace of spades, crossed to the king of hearts, and led a low spade to my king. But a fourth round of clubs promoted my partner's ten of spades as the contract-defeating winner.

My Tip for a Top

If either a ruff-and-sluff is useless to declarer or you are sure that you cannot take any tricks in the side suits, don't be afraid to give declarer a ruff-and-sluff. You may weaken his trump holding and develop one or more tricks for your side.

Chapter 8

The Short and the Long of it

> Good people all, of every sort,
>   Give ear unto my song;
> And if you find it wond'rous short,
>   It cannot hold you long.

> Elegy on the Death of a Mad Dog, *Oliver Goldsmith*

Bridge players often fall victim to ingrained habits. One of these occurs when declarer in a notrump contract is running a long suit and the defenders have to find one or more discards.

Beginners are taught not to discard from a four-card suit in which dummy or (more difficult to judge) the closed hand holds four or more cards. Fair enough, but when a defender holds a five-card suit, his Pavlovian reflex is to discard the fifth card at the first opportunity without further thought. Later, when the pressure mounts, he shows signs of distress, and an astute declarer can place the remaining cards without trouble and to his advantage.

My friend and team-mate, Mike Passell, called my attention to this phenomenon, and described these two hands from a Regional.

```
Dlr: South          ♠ Q 10
Vul: Both           ♡ A J 6
                    ◇ Q J 10 7 6
                    ♣ 7 6 2
    ♠ A 9 7 3                        ♠ J 6 2
    ♡ 7                              ♡ Q 9 8 5 4 3
    ◇ 5 2                            ◇ 9 4
    ♣ A J 10 9 8 4                   ♣ Q 3
                    ♠ K 8 5 4
                    ♡ K 10 2
                    ◇ A K 8 3
                    ♣ K 5
```

West	North	East	South
			1NT
Pass	3NT	Pass	Pass
Pass			

West led the ten of clubs, indicating zero or two higher honors, and East's queen was captured by declarer's king. South realized he would need to find the queen of hearts. Hoping for some informative discards, South trundled the diamonds.

Each defender had to make three discards. West selected a spade, a club and a further spade. East cooperated well by throwing two spades and a club. With no information to go by, South played a heart to the king and a heart. One down and a good board to Passell and his partner.

```
Dlr: West              ♠ Q 7 4
Vul: None              ♡ Q J 4
                       ◇ 6 5 4
                       ♣ A K 3 2
     ♠ K J 10 9 8                      ♠ 6 3
     ♡ K 3                             ♡ 10 9 8 5 2
     ◇ A J 3 2                         ◇ 10 9 8
     ♣ 6 4                             ♣ 8 7 5
                       ♠ A 5 2
                       ♡ A 7 6
                       ◇ K Q 7
                       ♣ Q J 10 9
```

West	North	East	South
1♠	Pass	Pass	1NT
Pass	2NT	Pass	3NT
Pass	Pass	Pass	

Passell led the ten of spades, again showing zero or two higher cards. As declarer was looking at 28 high-card points, West was marked with all the outstanding honors. Declarer's plan, as the heart finesse was sure to fail, was to run his club tricks, concede a trick to the ace of diamonds, and eventually endplay West to lead away from the king of hearts. However, Passell countered this line by discarding the three of hearts on the third round of clubs, followed by the two of diamonds. When declarer exited with the king of diamonds, East signaled with the ten. Passell exited with the king of spades, declarer won and cashed the queen of diamonds. Passell dropped the jack! Now South felt sure he was on the right track. He exited with a spade, but Passell, after cashing his spade tricks, suddenly produced the three of diamonds! One down.

My Tip for a Top

If you are defending and declarer starts running his long suit, don't automatically part with your "idle" long card. Consider discarding from your short suit first. It may mislead declarer, or at least put him to a tough guess.

Chapter 9

Unusual Defensive Moves

Cet animal est très méchant,
Quand on l'attaque il se défend.

This animal is very bad,
When attacked it defends itself.

Anon (La Ménagerie, *Theodore P.K.*)

Two basics rules that are taught to beginners fairly early in their bridge lives are:

1. Do not finesse against partner.

2. If, upon winning the first trick in a suit, you decide to return it and have two cards remaining, lead back the higher one.

As with all 'rules', these are not sacrosanct. A rare exception to the first occurs when one defender has no entries and suspects that declarer holds exactly one stopper in the suit led. In this case, he may play an encouraging lower card to the first trick. Gaining entry in the same suit later, he fires back his lowest card, allowing partner to kill declarer's potential second stopper.

Here is an illustration:

<pre>
                    Dummy
                    ♡ 7 6
    West   East
    ♡ K 10 9 4   ♡ A 5 2
                    Declarer
                    ♡ Q J 8 3
</pre>

West leads the ten of hearts against a notrump contract. East's ace of hearts is his only entry, and so if he wins the first trick and returns a heart, declarer plays an honor and West can neither win nor duck profitably. On this layout, East does better to put in his five at trick one, allowing declarer to win the trick. When West gets back in he can lead a heart to his partner's ace, and the defense will take three tricks in the suit.

Another well-known possibility is when third hand holds ace-queen-third and puts in the queen to stop the declarer holding up the king.

Sometimes the situation is less clear-cut.

Dummy
♡ 10 6

West   *East*
♡ K 9 5 2   ♡ A 8 3

Declarer
♡ Q J 7 4

West leads the two of hearts against a notrump contract. If dummy plays low, East can save a trick by inserting the eight. If dummy puts up the ten, East wins with the ace and returns the eight. West probably does best to duck his king.

The following deal from the 1984 Blue Ribbon Pairs shows that there are exceptions to the second rule as well.

Dlr: South   ♠ 8 3
Vul: E-W   ♡ K J 10 9
                   ◇ Q 10 9 4
                   ♣ Q 10 4

♠ Q 7 4 2   ♠ A J 9
♡ 8 4 3   ♡ 7 5 2
◇ A J 5 3   ◇ 7 6 2
♣ K 6   ♣ 9 8 7 3

                   ♠ K 10 6 5
                   ♡ A Q 6
                   ◇ K 8
                   ♣ A J 5 2

West	North	East	South
			1♣
Pass	1◇	Pass	1NT (a)
Pass	2NT	Pass	3NT
Pass	Pass	Pass	

(a) 15-17 points

West led the two of spades and dummy followed with the three. As can be seen, East has no possible entry outside the spade suit, and so he might play the jack to the first trick. But that could easily cost a trick if partner has led from ♠ K 10 4 2.

However, another interesting possibility was available. Win the first trick with the ace of spades and play back not the jack, as the rule says (and as was done at almost all tables), but the nine. This play was made by Peter Weichsel (and perhaps someone else), and was reported by Alan Truscott in his column in *The New York Times*. Declarer could still make the hand by a double-dummy line of play,[1] but not unnaturally went down, losing three spade tricks and one in each minor.

The routine return of the jack of spades was fatal to the defense. South won with the king and led the king of diamonds. West could win with the ace but couldn't play another spade without setting up South's ten. Two spade tricks, the ace of diamonds and the king of clubs were the limit for the defense.

There is an opportunity for the same type of defensive play in other situations where the opening leader's partner has no entries outside the suit led.

Dummy
♡ 8 4

West
♡ A 10 6 3

East
♡ K 9 2

Declarer
♡ Q J 7 5

When West leads the three of hearts East has two winning options: putting in the nine, and winning with the king and returning the two.

---

[1] Win with the king of spades and lead the king of diamonds. West wins with the ace, plays a spade to his partner's jack, and receives a club switch. Declarer rises with the ace, finesses the ten of diamonds, and cashes four rounds of hearts, squeezing West in three suits.

Here is a further interesting example.

Dlr: North   ♠ 9 6 3
Vul: None   ♡ Q 8 4
                      ◇ K J 10 6
                      ♣ J 9 4
                                          ♠ 8 7 5 2
                                          ♡ 10 7 6
                                          ◇ 9 8 3
                                          ♣ A 10 8

West	North	East	South
	Pass	Pass	1NT (a)
Dble	Pass	Pass	Pass

(a) 12-14 points

West leads the two of clubs, fourth best, and dummy puts in the nine. How do you plan the defense?

Sitting East was Lorraine Boyd, who has played several times for the New Zealand women's team. The normal play would be to go up with the ace and return the ten, catering for declarer holding king-third and clarifying the situation for partner. However, here Boyd realized the necessity to retain the ace as a later entry, and smoothly put in the ten.

This was the full deal:

Dlr: North   ♠ 9 6 3
Vul: None   ♡ Q 8 4
                      ◇ K J 10 6
                      ♣ J 9 4
♠ A K J   ♠ 8 7 5 2
♡ K J 3   ♡ 10 7 6
◇ Q 5 4   ◇ 9 8 3
♣ Q 7 5 2   ♣ A 10 8
                      ♠ Q 10 4
                      ♡ A 9 5 2
                      ◇ A 7 2
                      ♣ K 6 3

Declarer won the first trick with the king, finessed the ten of diamonds, cashed three more diamond tricks, East throwing a spade and South and West hearts, and cast off with a club. Boyd was able to win the trick with the eight, play a spade through declarer's queen, regain the lead with the ace of clubs and return a heart, leaving declarer with just six tricks. A pretty defense to justify West's aggressive double. And note that if East puts up the ace of clubs at trick one and returns a club, it is not difficult for declarer to endplay West into conceding two major-suit tricks.

My Tip for a Top

When your only entry in a notrump contract is in the suit led *and* declarer is marked with a four-card holding, consider, after winning the first trick, leading back your *lower* remaining card. Keeping your higher spot-card may be vital.

If declarer is marked with a three-card holding, you have useful intermediates and no side entry, consider playing one of those good spot-cards, retaining your winner for later in the play when it might be of greater use.

Chapter 10

A Bicycle Made for Two

El socialismo puede llegar solo en bicicleta.

Socialism can only arrive by bicycle.

José Antonio Viera Gallo

The racing tandem is a far cry from the old-fashioned bicycle for two. On the latter, any two people may go for a ride. The racing machine requires the cyclists to work together in tempo; in the same way that the conductor and orchestra are attuned to each other during a successful performance.

The same is true for defenders at the bridge table. When you are playing the dummy, you are alone, seeing all your resources exposed and concentrating on how best to deploy them.

But as a defender you have a partner whose strength and distribution are hidden, and you have to analyze and assume, deduce and discern, the complete layout from the bidding, the play and the signals you receive.

Very early, advancing players are introduced to the Wonderland of Signals, flashing neon signs in the darkness of defensive labyrinths. Signals are designed to help in deciding when to hold up in order to cut off declarer from his dummy; or what to keep in order to thwart an impending squeeze; or what to return to obtain a ruff. Very nice if you are on the receiving end, but what about poor partner groping in the dark?

Most players are so occupied with their thoughts, so engrossed in their own problems, that they look only at their cards, failing to visualize and appreciate partner's problems and dilemmas.

I look at a well-bid or well-defended hand — and I am sure many experts share my point of view — as a form of art providing the players with the same kind of satisfaction as the creative artist derives from the contemplation of his finished work.

When I look back on an artfully executed harmonious defense, I cannot help being reminded of the thoughts of the late Leonard Bernstein. Each play follows inevitably the previous one, leading to the dénouement, just as every note in its pure clarity blends into the harmony of the next one as Beethoven's Fifth Symphony.

Here is an example, which occurred at our 1957 Mexican Nationals. The protagonists were the eventual winners of the Open Pair event, Julius Rosenblum and Constant Fua, my long-standing friend and partner in Mexico.

This was the deal:

```
Dlr: North          ♠ K J 10
Vul: E-W            ♡ 9 7 4
                    ◇ 10 8 5 4
                    ♣ A Q 10
      ♠ 7 5 4                       ♠ A Q 9 8 3
      ♡ K 10 2                      ♡ 5 3
      ◇ K 2                         ◇ A J 9
      ♣ 8 6 5 4 3                   ♣ J 7 2
                    ♠ 6 2
                    ♡ A Q J 8 6
                    ◇ Q 7 6 3
                    ♣ K 9
```

West	North	East	South
	Pass	1♠	2♡
2♠	3♡	Pass	Pass
Pass			

Fua, in the West position, led the four of spades, and Rosenblum won with the queen. Correctly sizing up his chances, East returned the jack of diamonds, underleading his ace for the surrounding play. Declarer covered with the queen, and the defenders took three diamond tricks, West discarding a spade on the last. East continued with the ace and another spade. South ruffed with the queen of hearts, but Fua didn't fall into the trap of overruffing, which would have cost a trick. Eventually he made two more trump tricks for three down and a top.

I saved this hand as an example of beautiful defensive cooperation.

My Tip for a Top

When defending don't get lost in your own problems, think of your partner and try to visualize his hand. This will help you to assist him in solving his dilemmas. Remember: the bicycle you are riding is made for two!

Chapter 11

Lead that Fourth Suit!

It is not easy to make a simile go on all fours.

John Bunyan, *Lord Macaulay*

Even at the highest levels of expertise, blind opening leads present a problem — despite the maxim that there are no blind opening leads, only deaf bridge players!

In the past I have often pointed out the importance of listening to both partner's and the opponents' bidding. Even at the danger of being repetitious, the importance of this advice cannot be over-emphasized.

Here are two telling examples. In both cases, you are sitting West with both sides vulnerable.

1. You hold

♠ 5 3   ♡ A 10 9   ♢ 10 8 6 5 4   ♣ 7 4 2

The bidding proceeds as follows:

West	North	East	South
		1♡	1♠
Pass	2♡ (a)	3♣	4♠
Pass	Pass	Dble	Pass
Pass	Pass		

(a) A limit raise or better in spades

What is your lead?

2. Your hand is

$$\spadesuit\ Q\ 7\ 4 \quad \heartsuit\ Q\ 7\ 4\ 2 \quad \diamondsuit\ A\ 5\ 4 \quad \clubsuit\ Q\ 8\ 3$$

The auction goes like this:

West	North	East	South
			1♠
Pass	2♣	2NT (a)	3♠
4♡	4♠	Dble	Pass
Pass	Pass		

(a) Unusual for the red suits

What is your opening salvo this time?

The first hand occurred during the Master Pairs at the 1989 Mexican Nationals. If you led a heart without thinking, you blew your chance to defeat the contract.

This was the full deal:

Dlr: East
Vul: Both

```
                     ♠ A J 8
                     ♡ Q J 8 2
                     ◇ K 3 2
                     ♣ 9 8 3
   ♠ 5 3                                ♠ 9 4 2
   ♡ A 10 9                             ♡ K 6 5 4 3
   ◇ 10 8 6 5 4                         ◇ —
   ♣ 7 4 2                              ♣ A K J 10 6
                     ♠ K Q 10 7 6
                     ♡ 7
                     ◇ A Q J 9 7
                     ♣ Q 5
```

As my partner, Eddie Wold, had bid two suits and doubled the third, I expected him to be void in the fourth suit, diamonds. And as my entry was in the higher-ranking of the two side suits, I led the ten of diamonds as a suit preference signal.

As you can see, everything worked as planned. Wold ruffed the opening lead with the nine of spades, starting an echo to show three trumps. A heart to the ace, another diamond ruff and two top clubs produced a two-trick set.

Plus 500 proved to be a shared top. At most tables West led the ace of hearts with sad consequences for the defenders.

The second exhibit came from the Swiss team event at the same tournament. This was the full deal:

```
Dlr: South          ♠ K 9 8
Vul: Both           ♡ 8 3
                    ◇ 9 6
                    ♣ A J 10 9 6 2
   ♠ Q 7 4                          ♠ 5 2
   ♡ Q 7 4 2                        ♡ A 10 9 6 5
   ◇ A 5 4                          ◇ Q J 10 7 3 2
   ♣ Q 8 3                          ♣ —
                    ♠ A J 10 6 3
                    ♡ K J
                    ◇ K 8
                    ♣ K 7 5 4
```

East had shown two suits and doubled the third, so West led a club. And he selected the three to indicate an entry in diamonds, the lower-ranking of the remaining suits. East ruffed and returned the queen of diamonds. Thus the defense scored one heart, two diamonds and two club ruffs for plus 500.

My Tip for a Top

Listen to the bidding. If your partner shows two suits and then doubles the opponents' contract, lead the fourth suit.

Chapter 12

Unusual Suit Preference Signals

Matrimonial devotion
Doesn't seem to suit her notion.

The Mikado, *W.S. Gilbert*

Good defenders don't grow on trees. They develop as the result of hard work, endless discussions, experimentation by trial and error, and the careful deployment of signals.

Among the last facet, suit preference signals are the expert's favorite tool. They are used profusely by a top-notch partnership to avoid the lurking traps set by declarer.

I discussed some applications of these signals in both the previous chapter and *Tips for Tops*. However, in a Regional tournament in Victoria, B.C., two lesser-known situations turned up. Using the right tools, the defenders were able to achieve superior scores to those who were less well armed.

The first example occurred during the Flighted Open Pairs.

Dlr: West
Vul: None

	♠ K 10 8 2	
	♡ A 7 2	
	◇ K 10 6	
	♣ A J 5	
♠ A		♠ Q 5 3
♡ 5 4		♡ J 10 9 6 3
◇ A Q J 7 3 2		◇ 8
♣ K Q 10 4		♣ 7 6 3 2
	♠ J 9 7 6 4	
	♡ K Q 8	
	◇ 9 5 4	
	♣ 9 8	

West	North	East	South
1◇	Dble	1♡	1♠
2♣	2♠	Pass	Pass
3◇	3♠	Pass	Pass
Dble	Pass	Pass	Pass

Most Norths would overcall one notrump rather than double, but this time the latter worked all right. However, perhaps North should double three diamonds, having already announced his spade support. Here, South would pass and they would collect 100; but with no defense he would remove to three spades.

West, Mike Passell, led the king of clubs. Declarer played low from the dummy, and East discouraged with the seven, an upside-down signal. Accurately, Passell switched to the ace and another diamond. However, how could Passell tell partner that his entry was in the trump suit? Normally, a suit preference signal refers only to the side suits. But here a heart return would cost a trick, permitting declarer to win in hand, finesse the jack of clubs and discard his last diamond on the ace of clubs.

In situations where an entry in one of the side suits is clearly excluded, as in the club suit here, a cute gimmick solves the problem. A suit preference signal which asks for the return of the useless suit flags the command for a trump shift; whereas the remaining signal requests the return of the other side suit.

Passell led the jack of diamonds at trick three, and East ruffed away dummy's king. Back came a spade to the ace, the queen of diamonds was cashed, and a fourth round of diamonds promoted the queen of spades. Plus 300 and a top for East-West.

Another way of tackling this problem is simply to ignore the impossible suit, and to treat the trump suit as a side suit for suit preference purposes. Thus, in the present case, the queen of diamonds would ask for a trump return, and the jack of diamonds for a heart switch. Decide which method you prefer and discuss it with your partner.

The second situation is more frequent. Partner has bid a suit and you lead an honor from either known shortage or known length. In the former case, if your lead is a singleton, you would like to know which suit to shift to. In the latter case, you are not expecting to cash more than one trick in the suit and would like guidance, both from the dummy and partner, as to the best trick-two switch.

Partner makes life easy by playing a suit preference card at trick one, indicating where his entry lies.

Here is a beautiful example of partnership cooperation from the Master's Pairs in Victoria.

Dlr: East   ♠ Q
Vul: Both   ♡ 10 9 8 7 4
                                   ◇ K 10 6 5
                                   ♣ 9 8 5

♠ 9 8 7 5   ♠ K J 6 4
♡ Q 6 5   ♡ A 2
◇ J 9 8 7 2   ◇ 4
♣ K   ♣ A J 10 6 4 2

                                   ♠ A 10 3 2
                                   ♡ K J 3
                                   ◇ A Q 3
                                   ♣ Q 7 3

West	North		East	South
			1♣	1NT
Pass	2◇	(a)	Pass	2♡
Pass	Pass		Pass	

(a) Transfer bid

West led the king of clubs, and East, Eddie Wold, played the two as a suit preference signal. The seven of diamonds followed, won by dummy's king. Declarer called for the ten of hearts, but East went in with the ace, cashed the ace of clubs, and continued with the four of clubs, another request for the diamond suit. West ruffed, then led the two of diamonds. East trumped and played a fourth round of clubs, allowing West to make another trick with the queen of hearts. Plus 100 was a near top for East-West.

My Tip for a Top

Familiarize yourself with the diverse suit preference situations which occur with some regularity. Discuss your approach with your regular partner; you will reap handsome profits.

Chapter 13

Keeping Parity

What is a communist? One who hath yearnings
For equal division of unequal earnings.

Epigram, *Ebenezer Elliott*

The other day an eager student of the game accosted me: "What is this deal of keeping parity? The only thing which comes to my mind is the weakening dollar versus the German mark and the Swiss franc. I found no entry in the *Official Encyclopedia of Bridge*, so I consulted Webster's *New World Dictionary*. It carries no less than four definitions of parity. The most applicable to bridge says: 'The state or condition of being the same in power, value, rank, etc.; equality.' Please explain; I'm confused."

"Actually the answer is simple," I replied. "Just substitute *equal length* for parity and you will easily understand. The bridge meaning of keeping parity is to retain equal length with an opponent; that is, to keep the same number of cards in a suit as the dummy or — but this is more difficult as you cannot always know the exact length — the declarer. In most pertinent situations, it will come down to not discarding the fourth card in a suit in which the declarer's side also has four-card length."

If the defender fails to retain equal length, the consequences may be serious, as shown in the following deal from a club duplicate.

Dlr: South   ♠ K 9 4
Vul: E-W   ♡ 7 4
                              ◇ J 8 6 5
                              ♣ A Q 8 5
                                                  ♠ Q 7 2
                                                  ♡ 10 8 3
                                                  ◇ 9 7 4 3
                                                  ♣ K 7 2

West	North	East	South
			1NT (a)
Pass	3NT	Pass	Pass
Pass			

(a) 15-17 points

Your partner leads the queen of hearts, you play an encouraging eight, and declarer wins with the king. South runs the jack of clubs to your king, partner dropping the three. You return the ten of hearts. Declarer ducks, West overtakes with the jack, and dislodges declarer's ace with the nine of hearts, dummy shedding a low spade. Everyone follows as declarer plays a club to the ten and one back to the queen. What do you discard on dummy's last club?

Reluctant to pitch down to a doubleton queen of spades, East released the three of diamonds. This proved to be fatal as declarer cashed the ace and king of diamonds, dropping West's queen-ten doubleton. Dummy's eight of diamonds became the ninth trick for the game contract as the complete deal was:

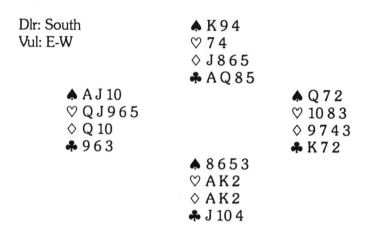

Dlr: South
Vul: E-W

♠ K 9 4
♡ 7 4
◇ J 8 6 5
♣ A Q 8 5

♠ A J 10
♡ Q J 9 6 5
◇ Q 10
♣ 9 6 3

♠ Q 7 2
♡ 10 8 3
◇ 9 7 4 3
♣ K 7 2

♠ 8 6 5 3
♡ A K 2
◇ A K 2
♣ J 10 4

Did East make a mistake in discarding the fourth diamond instead of the two of spades? Obviously he violated the rule of keeping parity — equal length — with the dummy. But there were also two other clues. South's distribution was likely to be 4-3-3-3 with four spades. If partner did not have at least the jack of spades, declarer always had nine tricks, thanks to the winning spade finesse. Another more subtle clue, but the hallmark of expert defenders, was the size of West's heart spot at trick four: the nine, a high heart. This card tried to signal an entry in the higher-ranking of the two remaining suits, namely spades. As declarer had the bare ace of hearts (or just possibly the ace-three) left, West could have returned a lower heart to indicate that he held a possible entry in the lower-ranking suit, diamonds.

On that hand, it was important to keep four to the nine. Now a hand from a pair game at a New York club where retaining four to the eight was critical.

Dlr: South   ♠ A 7 6 3
Vul: Both   ♡ 4 3
                              ◇ K 5 4
                              ♣ A Q 10 8

♠ Q J 10 8   ♠ K 9 5
♡ 8 6 5 2   ♡ Q 10 9
◇ J 7 6   ◇ Q 10 8
♣ 9 4   ♣ 7 6 3 2

                              ♠ 4 2
                              ♡ A K J 7
                              ◇ A 9 3 2
                              ♣ K J 5

West	North	East	South
			1NT
Pass	2♣	Pass	2♡
Pass	3NT	Pass	Pass
Pass			

West led the queen of spades. Declarer won with dummy's ace on the third round, then ran his club tricks. Thinking his hearts were useless, West discarded the two and five. Reading his opponent well (a good player sitting West *might* come down to a doubleton queen), declarer finessed the jack of hearts, and collected two valuable overtricks.

This was particularly poor defense by West when he knew that declarer had four hearts from the Stayman auction.

Which is the weakest four-card holding that could be worth a trick? The second-weakest possible! Suppose on the above deal the heart suit was distributed like this:

                         Dummy
                         ♡ 8 7
        West   *East*
        ♡ 6 4 3 2   ♡ Q 10 9
                         Declarer
                         ♡ A K J 5

As long as West holds all his hearts, the six will beat the five on the fourth round.

My Tip for a Top

Try to retain the same number of cards as an opponent in any suit — unless, of course, you cannot possibly win a trick in the suit whatever the distribution of the other cards.

If you are trying to retain parity in two suits but are forced to discard from one of them, discard from the suit on your *left*. It is a principle of squeeze defense to try to retain your guard in the suit on your right. This way, if declarer abandons that suit, you can do so as well as you are discarding after him.

Chapter 14

Decide the Fate of the Contract

Why, I hold fate
Clasp'd in my fist, and could command the course
Of time's eternal motion, hadst thou been
One thought more steady than an ebbing sea.

'Tis Pity She's a Whore, *John Ford*

The final contract has been reached, the opening lead made and the dummy tabled. The defenders know their goal, but how should their assessment of the contract affect their play?

Arguably the most important thing for the defenders to decide is the fate of the contract. If they judge that it should go down, they should signal accurately to make sure they do defeat it. However, if they judge that the declarer will make the contract only if he can work out the right line, they shouldn't signal at all, leaving declarer to control his own destiny. (A similar principle applies when trying to stop an overtrick or two on a hand from a pair tournament.)

Here is a hand from the 1991 Cap Gemini Pandata World Top Tournament.

Dlr: South
Vul: N-S

```
                        ♠ Q 10 9 6 5
                        ♡ 6 4
                        ♦ A Q 9 6
                        ♣ K 2
     ♠ K 8                              ♠ J 7 4
     ♡ 7                                ♡ 10 8 2
     ♦ K 8 7 5 3                        ♦ J 10 4 2
     ♣ J 8 7 5 3                        ♣ Q 10 9
                        ♠ A 3 2
                        ♡ A K Q J 9 5 3
                        ♦ —
                        ♣ A 6 4
```

West	North	East	South
			2♣
Pass	2♦	Pass	2♡
Pass	2♠	Pass	3♡
Pass	4NT (a)	Pass	5♣ (b)
Pass	5NT	Pass	7♡
Pass	Pass	Pass	

(a) Roman Key Card Blackwood
(b) Four key cards

The declarer was the mercurial Brazilian, Gabriel Chagas. West led a low club, and declarer won with dummy's king, played a club to the ace, ruffed his club loser in the dummy, and ran his seven trump tricks.

With one heart remaining, West had king doubleton in both spades and diamonds. Dummy had the ace-queen of diamonds and queen-ten of spades. Which card should West throw when the final trump is led?

Obviously, it depends upon South's remaining cards! If South has the ace-jack of spades and a diamond, West must throw a spade to give declarer a guess. But with the actual layout, West must discard a diamond.

At the time, West discarded a spade, baring his king and allowing the grand slam to make. If only East had realized that they should be defeating the grand slam, he would have discarded in such a way as to give his partner the count. The simple approach is to throw all his spades. Another is to use the Vinje Trump Signal, which works very well on this type of hand. East plays high-low in the trump suit to show he has a hand with three suits containing an odd number of cards and one containing an even number (a void counting as even). Here, that makes it easy for West to count out the hand. But it must be added that on most hands declarer benefits more from the Vinje Trump Signal than do the defenders.

If you are sure declarer will make the hand if left to himself, try to find a play that might deflect him from his normal course. Tim Seres, the great Australian player, used this theme in his *Bols* Bridge Tip. His article didn't concentrate on the textbook deceptive plays, rather on finding an unusual thrust. This was the deal he gave:

Dlr: South   ♠ A K Q 4
Vul: Both   ♡ Q 10 7
                     ♢ 7 6 5
                     ♣ 8 4 2

♠ 8 7 3   ♠ J 10 5
♡ 8 6 4 3   ♡ A J 9
♢ 10 9   ♢ Q J 8 3 2
♣ J 9 7 5   ♣ Q 10

                   ♠ 9 6 2
                   ♡ K 5 2
                   ♢ A K 4
                   ♣ A K 6 3

West	North	East	South
			1NT
Pass	2♣	Pass	2♢
Pass	3NT	Pass	Pass
Pass			

West led the ten of diamonds. In a top-flight pair event, every declarer but one made his contract with two club, two diamond, one heart and four spade tricks. But at the last table South won the diamond lead and immediately started to cash the spades. Under the ace and king, East dropped the ten and jack! Expecting the suit to be dividing 4-2, South played a low spade to his nine. But now declarer had to find an entry to the dummy. He led the king of hearts, which East ducked.

At this point, declarer could have got home with an endplay, cashing his minor-suit winners and exiting with a diamond. But he led a low heart and finessed dummy's ten. When that lost to the jack, he was destined to finish one down.

Here is a hand from an international pair tournament that shows you must never play "automatically."

```
Dlr: East              ♠ A 9 7 2
Vul: N-S               ♡ Q 10
                       ◇ A Q
                       ♣ K 7 6 5 2
     ♠ 5                                 ♠ K 6
     ♡ J 9 8 6 5 3 2                     ♡ A K 7 4
     ◇ 8 7 4                             ◇ 10 9 6 2
     ♣ Q 3                               ♣ 10 9 8
                       ♠ Q J 10 8 4 3
                       ♡ —
                       ◇ K J 5 3
                       ♣ A J 4
```

West	North	East	South
		Pass	1♠
Pass	3♣	Pass	3◇
Pass	3♠	Pass	4♣
Pass	4◇	Pass	4♡
Pass	4♠	Pass	6♠
Pass	Pass	Pass	

West led the six of hearts and East played the *king*. South ruffed and finessed the queen of spades, losing to East's king.

Now it was clear to declarer that West had the queen of clubs. If East held that card, he would have had twelve points and surely would have opened the bidding. So South drew the last trump and eschewed the club finesse. When the queen dropped, the slam was home.

Who was the declarer? The inimitable Rixi Markus. As she said, if East had played the *ace* of hearts at trick one, she would have taken the club finesse and gone down.

In fact, East can do even better. After playing the ace of hearts (how can that play cost?) and winning trick two with the king of spades, East should return a *low* heart to reinforce the picture in South's mind.

My Tip for a Top

When defending, as quickly as possible try to judge the likely outcome of the contract. If you think it should be defeated (or, in a matchpointed pair event, not conceded with an unnecessary overtrick or two), signal accurately to make sure you get all your tricks. But if you think it will depend on how well declarer guesses the lie of the cards, don't help him with revealing signals.

Finally, especially when playing in an imp game, if you see a chance to divert declarer from the straight and narrow path, take it. It is surprising how often the appearance of an unexpected honor card can deflect a declarer.

Chapter 15

Pips for Profit

Quid sit futurum cras fuge quaerere et
Quem Fors dierum cumque dabit lucro
Appone.

Drop the question what tomorrow may bring,
and count as profit every day that Fate allows you.

Odes, *Horace*

After watching us for a whole session at a Regional, a kibitzer asked me for the reasons that make expert partnerships so successful on defense. I explained that, apart from technical skill and table presence that sometimes borders on ESP, the intelligent use of signals contributes most to expert success.

If you watch a top pair in action, you will be impressed by two things: the smooth tempo of their plays, and their judicious use of suit preference signals in critical situations.

Attitude and count signals are abundant in all circles, but suit preference signals, expressed by the order of play of non-honor cards, are badly neglected by the average defender. The expert, when it is critical, will transmit a message with every card.

To illustrate, here are three hands Eddie Wold and I played at a Sault Ste. Marie Regional. The first arose during the Knockout Teams.

Dlr: West   ♠ K Q 10 3
Vul: None   ♡ 10 8 4
                                   ◇ 10 8 7
                                   ♣ K 10 9
          ♠ A 9 5 2   ♠ 7 4
          ♡ A K 3   ♡ 9 7
          ◇ A 3   ◇ 9 6 5 4 2
          ♣ J 7 5 3   ♣ A 8 6 4
                                   ♠ J 8 6
                                   ♡ Q J 6 5 2
                                   ◇ K Q J
                                   ♣ Q 2

West	North	East	South
Wold		*Rosenkranz*	
1♣	Pass	Pass	1♡
1♠	2♡	Pass	Pass
Pass			

Wold led the five of spades, third- or fifth-best in our methods. We use upside-down count and attitude signals, but suit preference signals are employed regularly too.

I encouraged a continuation by playing the four (upside-down, remember), and declarer won in his hand with the jack. South immediately played a low trump, but Wold hopped up with the king to play the ace and another spade, which I ruffed.

Interpreting West's nine of spades as a suit preference signal, I obediently led my two of diamonds. Wold won with the ace and returned his second diamond. I played the four as another suit preference signal. Declarer persisted with a second round of trumps. West put up his ace and fired back the seven of clubs. I won with my ace and gave Wold a diamond ruff. Two down for a four-imp gain.

At the other table, West opened one notrump and went one down in this contract on the king-of-spades opening lead.

The next two hands occurred during the Open Pairs.

Dlr: East
Vul: E-W

```
                    ♠ 10 2
                    ♡ Q 4
                    ◇ Q J 10 9 2
                    ♣ A Q 7 6
   ♠ 9 8                           ♠ K 4 3
   ♡ A K J 6 5                     ♡ 10 8 7 2
   ◇ A 7 3                         ◇ 6 5
   ♣ 10 8 2                        ♣ K J 5 3
                    ♠ A Q J 7 6 5
                    ♡ 9 3
                    ◇ K 8 4
                    ♣ 9 4
```

West	North	East	South
Rosenkranz		Wold	
		Pass	1♠
2♡	Dble (a)	3♡	3♠
Pass	4♠	Pass	Pass
Pass			

(a) Negative

I started off with the king of hearts. East gave upside-down count with the two, the attitude being known as the queen was nestling in the dummy. The ace of hearts fetched the opponents' remaining hearts, while Wold signaled with the seven, the lowest outstanding heart.

This was an absolutely essential suit preference signal for a club shift, and accordingly I switched to the two of clubs. Declarer finessed dummy's queen and East won the trick with his king. The defenders still had to come to the ace of diamonds for one down.

Notice that on a diamond shift at trick three declarer easily makes his contract. He wins the second diamond in dummy, having unblocked his king under West's ace. South finesses East's king of spades, draws all the trumps, and discards his losing club on dummy's established diamonds.

Suppose that East's king of clubs is exchanged for the king of diamonds. Then East signals at trick two with the ten of hearts, suggesting a diamond shift. This might be critical if declarer holds three clubs and only two diamonds, because then he can discard a diamond loser on dummy's fourth club after the trump suit has been successfully negotiated for no losers.

This final exhibit is more subtle, but it is good demonstration of harmonious defensive collaboration.

```
Dlr: East                    ♠ K Q 8 2
Vul: E-W                     ♡ K 8 7
                             ◇ K 8 3
                             ♣ A 8 2
         ♠ 7 6                                  ♠ A 9 5
         ♡ Q 10 6 3                             ♡ A 5 4
         ◇ 9 7 6                                ◇ A Q 5 4 2
         ♣ J 10 7 4                             ♣ 9 6
                             ♠ J 10 4 3
                             ♡ J 9 2
                             ◇ J 10
                             ♣ K Q 5 3
```

West	North	East	South
Rosenkranz		*Wold*	
		1 ◇	Pass
Pass	Dble	Pass	1 ♠
Pass	2 ♠	Pass	4 ♠
Pass	Pass	Pass	

I led my third-best diamond, the six, to indicate that I held three (or four) cards in partner's suit. Wold won with the queen and South dropped the jack. With all the low diamonds in sight, East could diagnose the position and cashed his ace of diamonds.

I now made the key play: the nine of diamonds, an unnecessarily high pip to show partner that I had a little something in the higher-ranking of two remaining suits: hearts.

Wold now knew it was safe to lead a third round of diamonds to dummy's king, on which declarer discarded his two of hearts. South started to pull trumps. East won the second round with his ace, then exited with the nine of spades, on which I discarded the three of hearts.

Declarer tried a tricky play and led a low heart from dummy, hoping to induce Wold to rise with his ace in case South had blanked his queen of hearts. But my partner was not to be deceived, helped by my signal at trick two. He smoothly contributed his two of hearts, and my queen topped declarer's jack. Thus the ambitious contract was defeated by two tricks for a near top score.

My Tip for a Top

If you want to improve your defense substantially:
   Watch carefully the pips of the cards played by your side.
   Use them to send or receive suit preference signals when necessary.

Chapter 16

The Recovery Play

There is only the fight to recover what has been lost
And found and lost again and again; and now, under conditions
That seems unpropitious. But perhaps neither gain nor loss.
For us, there is only the trying. The rest is not our business.

East Coker, *T.S. Eliot*

I t is a pity that bridge players nowadays know so little about the
old-time greats. And worse — with few exceptions — they are
not even interested in their exploits. During my active career, I was
lucky to meet quite a few of them and learn some valuable lessons
at and away from the bridge table.

I remember many years ago asking Johnny Crawford for advice
about how to play successful matchpoint bridge. He summed up
his philosophy neatly: "If you want to be a consistent winner in
matchpointed events, George, buy yourself a big basket, put it
under the table and just pick up the points your opponents chuck
away. Remember, don't do anything fancy. Just sit still and the wins
will come rolling in."

Many consistent winners like Kaplan, Kay and Silodor, to name
but a few, share this view. A below-average score was something to
be avoided if possible, but when it happened you took it with quiet
resignation, knowing it was part of the game and that the rare bad
result would be amply compensated by good bidding and play on
other deals.

However, there was another school of experts who thought
differently. My mentor, the great Johnny Gerber, was perhaps the
most successful representative of this minority. When Gerber felt he
was heading for a below-average score, he went out of his way to
change things around. A true gambler by nature, he was always
ready to risk his probable three matchpoints (on a twelve top) for a
cold zero if he had any chance to recover and produce a near-top
board. The following deal is an eloquent testimony to Gerber's
brilliance.

Dlr: South   ♠ 10 9 5 4
Vul: None   ♡ A J
                      ◇ 8 5 4
                      ♣ 10 9 8 3

♠ J 8 6 2	♠ K 7
♡ K Q 8 3	♡ 9 5 4 2
◇ K 6	◇ 9 3 2
♣ 7 5 4	♣ K J 6 2

                      ♠ A Q 3
                      ♡ 10 7 6
                      ◇ A Q J 10 7
                      ♣ A Q

West	North	East	South
			2NT
Pass	3♣	Pass	3◇
Pass	3NT	Pass	Pass
Pass			

Gerber, sitting West, led the three of hearts, won with dummy's jack. Declarer immediately set out to establish his diamond suit, finessing the queen. At this point our expert, wrongly as it turns out, thought his opening lead had given away a trick. Judging that heroic measures were called for, he ducked the diamond with his doubleton king!

Thinking his finesse had worked, the happy declarer returned to dummy with a heart and repeated the "proven" diamond finesse — and the roof fell in. Gerber won with the king of diamonds and cashed his top hearts. When South discarded his low spade, Gerber exited with a spade, and East had to score the king of clubs at the end.

The contract made, but the declarer got a poor score. At most tables, West led a spade, giving declarer a free finesse. The declarer gave up a diamond and ended with an overtrick.

Playing with Eddie Wold in the Open Pairs at the 1986 Mexican Nationals, this deal came up:

Dlr: South

Vul: None

```
                         ♠ A 7
                         ♡ K J 8 6
                         ◇ K 10 3
                         ♣ 10 6 3 2
     ♠ J 4 3 2                              ♠ Q 10 9 5
     ♡ Q 3 2                                ♡ 9 5 4
     ◇ Q J 9 5                              ◇ 8 7 6
     ♣ 5 4                                  ♣ A 8 7
                         ♠ K 8 6
                         ♡ A 10 7
                         ◇ A 4 2
                         ♣ K Q J 9
```

West	North	East	South
			1NT
Pass	2♣	Pass	2◇
Pass	3NT	Pass	Pass
Pass			

I led the normal queen of diamonds, only to find that I had given away a trick. Declarer won with the ace of diamonds and started to establish his club tricks. Suddenly Johnny Gerber came to mind. Declarer rated to have the ace of hearts, and so my queen was dead unless South had the ten as well. Thus I discarded the two of hearts on the third round of clubs.

My partner returned a diamond, won in the dummy. On the fourth club, I parted with a spade. Persuaded by my discard, declarer continued with the king of hearts and a heart to the ten, losing to my bare queen.

This gave us an over-average score as many Wests selected the same opening lead. I should have expected that and perhaps not been so worried about trying to gain a trick by abnormal means later in the play. But my play was still reasonable. It was my best chance to generate an extra trick.

My Tip for a Top

If you have made an unfavorable opening lead and are contemplating an unusual action in an effort to recover the trick lost, ask yourself:

Was my choice really disastrous, or will I have company?

How is our game; can we afford a below-average score?

Am I a gambler by nature; will I be doubly sorry if the second adventure backfires?

And perhaps most important of all: How will my partner react to my action, especially if it doesn't work? How will it affect our partnership?

Chapter 17

Don't Panic, Keep Your Cool

Here is wine,
Alive with sparkles — never, I aver,
Since Ariadne was a vintager,
So cool a purple.

Endymion, *John Keats*

Psychology has always been an important weapon in the expert's arsenal, but I hardly suspected that knowledge of physiology can also be useful. I am of course referring to the famous experiments on conditioned reflexes by the Russian Nobel Prize winner physiologist, Ivan Pavlov.

Let me introduce you to a quasi-Pavlovian reflex common to most bridge players. You will recognize this familiar scene: The opening leader gets off to a lead that allows the declarer to take a couple of fast discards. When finally the defending side gets in, the Pavlovian reflex occurs: with lightning speed — and most of the time without thinking — the defender tables a card of the suit from which declarer discarded. A little thinking will tell you that there is no longer a need to rush. If there was damage, it is already done; attacking another suit may be more productive, and there may still be a way to beat the contract.

Here are two examples. Kibitzing a Monday evening club game, I witnessed the following:

Dlr: South
Vul: None

```
                    ♠ 9 8 6 3 2
                    ♡ J 2
                    ◇ A K Q
                    ♣ 8 4 3
     ♠ —                          ♠ Q J 10
     ♡ K 10 8 5 4                 ♡ A Q 3
     ◇ J 10 9 8                   ◇ 7 6 5 3 2
     ♣ K J 7 5                    ♣ 9 2
                    ♠ A K 7 5 4
                    ♡ 9 7 6
                    ◇ 4
                    ♣ A Q 10 6
```

West	North	East	South
			1♠
Dble (a)	2NT (b)	3◇	4♠
Pass	Pass	Dble	Pass
Pass	Pass		

(a) Not the strongest take-out double in history
(b) Spade fit, defensive values

West got off to the normal lead of the jack of diamonds, and declarer continued with two more high diamonds, ridding himself of the six and seven of hearts. Then South cashed two high trumps, West discarding the four and five of hearts. When East gained the lead with the queen of spades, he succumbed to the Pavlov reflex: he cashed the ace of hearts and followed with the queen of hearts. Declarer ruffed and, in no doubt about the position of the king of clubs, led the queen of clubs from his hand.

West was hopelessly endplayed. A club return would be into declarer's ace-ten tenace, and a red-suit return would give a ruff-and-discard, allowing North to get rid of a club loser.

When in with the queen of spades, had East stopped to think he might have seen the advantage in leading a club. This would have foiled the endplay. When he regains the lead with the ace of hearts, another club lead through declarer would set the doubled contract by one trick.

Notice that on a heart lead the defense can take two hearts, one club and one high trump, again just a one-trick set.

So, by panicking, East blew the defense when he played two

rounds of hearts. Note also that West tried to help by discouraging in hearts. Even after cashing the ace of hearts, it wasn't too late to switch to clubs as West still had a safe heart exit.

A different variation occurred in a matchpoint event when I played in four spades from the South position after Edith raised my one-spade opening to three spades, and I went on to game.
    These were the four hands:

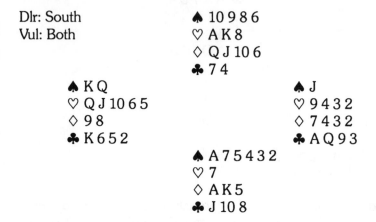

Dlr: South   ♠ 10 9 8 6
Vul: Both   ♡ A K 8
                   ◇ Q J 10 6
                   ♣ 7 4

♠ K Q   ♠ J
♡ Q J 10 6 5   ♡ 9 4 3 2
◇ 9 8   ◇ 7 4 3 2
♣ K 6 5 2   ♣ A Q 9 3

                   ♠ A 7 5 4 3 2
                   ♡ 7
                   ◇ A K 5
                   ♣ J 10 8

The opening lead of the queen of hearts was won in dummy. Noticing that a single club discard wouldn't help, I tried a deceptive play. I cashed dummy's other high heart and discarded the five of diamonds! I hoped that when the defense gained the lead they would automatically return a diamond: the suit from which I had discarded.
    Sure enough, after I played the ace and another trump, West won and without any hesitation switched to the nine of diamonds. Winning with the ace, I cashed the king of diamonds, then crossed to dummy with a trump. Two of my clubs went away on dummy's queen and jack of diamonds. The overtrick was worth a near top; at nearly all the tables the defense came to one trump and two club tricks.

My Tip for a Top

If, after the opening lead, declarer takes a couple of quick discards, don't panic. When you gain the lead, don't automatically return the suit from which declarer has discarded. Reflect whether attacking a different suit may be more productive.

Chapter 18

Win with the Trump Ace in its Time

> Dost thou love life? Then do not squander time,
> for that's the stuff life is made of.

Poor Richard's Almanack, *Benjamin Franklin*

O ne of the most common mistakes of the average defender is to win without thought the first round of trumps with the ace.

Yet, curiously enough, the same defender has learned that it can be advisable to lead a small trump from ace- or king-third to cut down possible ruffs in dummy, and often applies this technique.

The ace of trumps is a valuable asset and should not be wasted thoughtlessly. There may be several reasons for not taking the trump ace at the first opportunity.

Alfred Sheinwold was the first, to my knowledge, to write a lengthy treatise on this subject in the late, lamented *Popular Bridge*.

Here are two typical examples from a Chicago Regional.

Dlr: South
Vul: E-W

	♠ K 8 3	
	♡ 10 8 6 5	
	◇ A Q J 8 3 2	
	♣ —	
♠ 6 2		♠ A 9 7
♡ 9 7 4 3		♡ K 2
◇ K 10 9		◇ 7 6 5 4
♣ A J 8 7		♣ Q 9 6 5
	♠ Q J 10 5 4	
	♡ A Q J	
	◇ —	
	♣ K 10 4 3 2	

West Rosenkranz	North	East Wold	South
			1♠
Pass	4♣ (a)	Pass	4♠
Pass	Pass	Pass	

(a) A splinter bid, not really recommended with only three trumps

The opening lead was the two of spades, the normal choice from two low trumps. Wold covered dummy's three with the seven, declarer winning with the ten. South ruffed a club in the dummy, took a successful heart finesse, and ruffed a second club in the dummy, Wold carefully unblocking his queen.

The next two plays were the ace of diamonds, for a club discard, and a second heart to the king and ace. Now declarer led the queen of spades to East's ace. Back came the nine of clubs, West's jack winning. West cashed the ace of clubs before returning a heart, which East ruffed with his remaining trump to defeat the contract.

Do I hear you say that had declarer known the king of hearts was doubleton, he could have made his contract by a loser-on-loser play, leading the queen of diamonds from dummy and discarding the ten of clubs? It appears that West wins with the king of diamonds but the declarer loses only two more tricks: the two black aces.

This isn't so because West returns a heart instead of cashing his ace of clubs, and East still gets his heart ruff.

Notice the importance of not playing the ace of spades at trick one. Even if East rises with the ace and returns a trump at trick two, the extremely lucky lie of the cards allows declarer to fulfill his contract in many different ways. For example: He unblocks the ten of spades and wins East's trump return in dummy to lead the ace of diamonds followed by the queen of diamonds, discarding two clubs from the closed hand. West wins with the king but has no good riposte. A diamond return is won in dummy, the outstanding trump pulled with dummy's king, and South can claim the rest. A heart switch fares no better. Declarer wins the free finesse and draws trumps ending in the dummy.

Even returning the ace of clubs does not help the defense. Try to work it out for yourself.

The second hand was reported by Ira Chorush.

Dlr: South   ♠ J 5
Vul: None   ♡ 10 2
                              ◇ A K 3
                              ♣ A K 9 7 5 4

♠ 9 3 2   ♠ A 4
♡ A 8 7 6   ♡ Q J 9 3
◇ J 10 9 5   ◇ Q 8 7 6
♣ 10 8   ♣ J 6 3

                              ♠ K Q 10 8 7 6
                              ♡ K 5 4
                              ◇ 4 2
                              ♣ Q 2

West	North	East	South
			2♠
Pass	2NT	Pass	3♡ (a)
Pass	4♠	Pass	Pass
Pass			

(a) Maximum with a heart feature

The opening lead was the ten of clubs. Declarer won in his hand with the queen and led a spade to the jack. Chorush, sitting East, ducked! He reasoned correctly that if declarer held the ace of hearts, the contract was bound to succeed even if the opening lead were a singleton. (Also, West had played the two of spades on the first round of the suit, denying the ability to ruff a club.) Chorush realized that the only hope was to find South with king-third in hearts.

After winning the second round of trumps, Chorush led the queen of hearts to collect three heart tricks and defeat the contract.

Did declarer play the hand to best advantage? Suppose that instead of drawing trumps he tries to ruff one heart in dummy. He wins the first trick in the dummy and immediately leads a heart toward his king. West wins with the ace and returns a trump, which East must duck. A second round of hearts is won by East, who now cashes the ace of spades and a high heart to defeat the contract.

My Tip for a Top

When a trump is led and you hold the guarded ace, don't take it prematurely without a very good reason. The holdup can be the winning play in many situations.

Chapter 19

Appearances Can Be Deceptive

There is no trusting appearances.

The School for Scandal, *Richard Brinsley Sheridan*

Finally you have mastered the art of signaling. Carefully you watch the spot cards on partner's leads, plays and discards. Having scored a few successes in your regular game, you tend to relax and let the mechanics take over and guide you, like flying a plane on automatic pilot.

My advice is: Beware! You may be stepping into dangerous territory. Appearances are often deceiving, and to rely too much on signals or the fall of cards alone may induce you to forget about the whole picture. Pervasive laziness may take the place of common sense without your realizing it.

To illustrate my point, here are two hands I kibitzed. The first arose during the Knockout Teams at the 1986 Mexican Nationals.

Dlr: North
Vul: Both

	♠ K Q 10 6 3	
	♡ 9 7 6	
	◇ A 7 6	
	♣ A 6	
♠ 7		♠ J 9 4 2
♡ K Q 3		♡ J 8 4 2
◇ J 10 9 2		◇ 8 5 4
♣ 9 7 5 4 3		♣ K 8
	♠ A 8 5	
	♡ A 10 5	
	◇ K Q 3	
	♣ Q J 10 2	

West	North	East	South
			1NT
Pass	2♡ (a)	Pass	2♠
Pass	3NT	Pass	4♠
Pass	Pass	Pass	

(a) Transfer bid

The East-West seats were occupied by two of my talented pupils. They prided themselves on their defensive abilities. They used normal count and attitude signals, but Roman discards, third-and-fifth-highest leads, coded tens and nines (showing zero or two higher honors), and several suit preference signals completed their defensive armory.

West led the jack of diamonds, denying a higher honor. Declarer won with dummy's ace and played four rounds of spades, losing the last to East's jack. West discarded in order the four, seven and three of clubs, and declarer pitched the five of hearts.

East correctly returned the four of hearts, his third best, declarer winning with the ace and West dropping the three. South tried the club finesse, but it lost and East returned a ... diamond! The declarer promptly claimed an overtrick in his unmakable contract.

East had relied too heavily on his partner's "discouraging" heart signal. But a little counting would have made it clear that declarer, who had already shown up with sixteen points (the ace of spades, the ace of hearts, the king-queen of diamonds and the queen-jack of clubs), couldn't also hold the king-queen of hearts. East should have realized that West's three of hearts was a forced play. Also, West had tried to help his partner, discarding first a discouraging four of clubs and then a suit preference seven.

The second deal is from a Club Championship round in Mexico City in 1986.

```
Dlr: North                    ♠ A K
Vul: None                     ♡ A K 9 8 7
                              ◇ Q J 7 5
                              ♣ J 5
      ♠ Q 8 6 3                              ♠ J 7 5 4 2
      ♡ J 10                                 ♡ Q 6 4 3
      ◇ A 8 6 4 3                            ◇ K 2
      ♣ A Q                                  ♣ 8 7
                              ♠ 10 9
                              ♡ 5 2
                              ◇ 10 9
                              ♣ K 10 9 6 4 3 2
```

West	North	East	South
	1♡	Pass	Pass
Dble	Redble	1♠	2♣
2♠	3♣	3♠	4♣
Pass	Pass	Pass	

North's three clubs was certainly sporting! It is surprising South didn't bid game, but perhaps he knows his partner's style.

Sitting East was our leading pro, partnering one of his pupils. West led the normal three of spades. Declarer won in the dummy and cashed the ace-king of hearts, noticing with interest the fall of the ten and jack from West. He now tried the deceptive loser-on-loser play of the nine of hearts, intending to pitch a diamond, but our pro covered with the queen. Declarer ruffed with the nine of clubs and West overruffed with the queen.

West cashed the ace of diamonds, but when East dropped a "discouraging" two, he abandoned the suit and returned a spade. Declarer was home. He led the eight of hearts and discarded his losing diamond. West had to ruff with the ace of clubs.

West was thoughtlessly influenced by his partner's apparently discouraging two of diamonds. He did not stop to count and reason that East *must* hold the king of diamonds because with both minor-suit kings and long clubs, South would not have passed over his partner's one-heart opening bid. Furthermore, if South had the king of diamonds and not the king of clubs, he would have been playing trumps, not hearts.

My Tip for a Top

To become a good defender, keep track of the spots played and develop good signaling habits. *But* do not rely on them automatically and exclusively. Count as much as you can and try to form a picture of the declarer's hand.

Keep in mind that partner's carding might be forced; don't fall into the trap of deceptive appearances.

Chapter 20

No Rules are Cast in Iron

Habit rules the unreflecting mind.

Ecclesiastical Sonnets

In one's bridge childhood one is taught rules. Later, as childhood moves into adulthood, one learns that these axioms should not be treated as the gospel truth, and that there are times when they should be broken. The $64 question is: When should one ignore seemingly sound practices and violate reputable, longstanding tenets?

For example, in the middle of the hand you are on lead and are forced to break a new suit like J x x (x) or Q x x (x). Which card do you lead?

Your automatic reflex is to put a low card on the table. After all, a venerable saying dictates: "From three or four cards to an honor, lead low." But hold on — is that always right? *It depends; there isn't a simple yes-or-no answer.* Let us look at this suit diagram:

                    Dummy
                    ♠ A 10 3
    You   *Partner*
    ♠ Q 7 6 5   ♠ J 9 4 2
                    Declarer
                    ♠ K 8

Here it does not matter which card you lead; the opponents will make only two tricks. But change the layout to:

                    Dummy
                    ♠ A 10 3
    You   *Partner*
    ♠ Q 7 6 5   ♠ J 8 4 2
                    Declarer
                    ♠ K 9

Now if you lead a low card, partner has to put up his jack, and your queen can be finessed on the way back. But suppose you lead the queen. Now declarer cannot come to three tricks without an endplay. (And, of course, it is the same situation if you have the jack and partner the queen.)

This is also true if you strength the dummy:

Dummy
♠ A 10 9

You   *Partner*
♠ Q 7 6 5   ♠ J 4 3 2

Declarer
♠ K 8

You must lead the queen, not a low card.

You are faced with a more difficult decision if the dummy is on your right; but if you can see only two cards in the dummy, you must lead your honor. With three cards in the dummy on your right, you have to make an intelligent guess whether or not the closed hand has a doubleton. If this is a strong possibility, lead low. For example:

Dummy
♠ A 10 3

Partner   *You*
♠ J 7 6 5   ♠ Q 8 4 2

Declarer
♠ K 9

Declarer can take three tricks if you switch to the queen.

In other situations, though, lead your honor and make declarer guess whether you have led from Q J x (x), Q x x (x) or J x x (x).

Eddie Wold gave me this hand from a Regional.

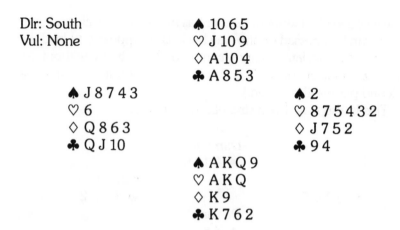

Dlr: South
Vul: None

Against South's contract of six notrump, Wold led the safe queen of clubs. Declarer won in hand and started to work on spades, unblocking dummy's ten on the second round as East discarded a heart. South cashed his three heart winners, West discarding a spade and a diamond, and then exited with the ace and another club to give this position:

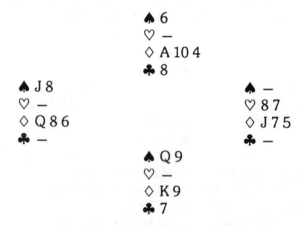

Declarer was hoping that West would be endplayed, and as you can see, the endplay works if West returns a *low* diamond. But Wold led the *queen* of diamonds and declarer was helpless.

The next hand comes from the Becker syndicated column. It was originally written up as featuring Sir Arthur Conan Doyle's most famous creations, Sherlock Holmes and Doctor Watson.

```
Dlr: North              ♠ K J 10 5
Vul: E-W                ♡ K J 9 2
                        ◇ K 3
                        ♣ A Q 4
        ♠ 7 6                           ♠ A Q 4 3
        ♡ 7 3                           ♡ A Q 6 4
        ◇ J 6 5                         ◇ Q 7 4 2
        ♣ 10 9 8 7 6 2                  ♣ 5
                        ♠ 9 8 2
                        ♡ 10 8 5
                        ◇ A 10 9 8
                        ♣ K J 3
```

West	North	East	South
	1♡	Pass	1NT
Pass	2NT	Pass	3NT
Pass	Pass	Pass	

West led the ten of clubs. Declarer won with the jack, then ran the nine of spades to Dr. Watson's queen. At this point Watson switched to the two of diamonds, giving declarer his contract when West wasn't farsighted enough to duck. But if Watson had returned the *queen* of diamonds, it would have defeated the contract for certain.

Declarer is marked with the king-jack of clubs and ace of diamonds from the bidding. If he has the jack of diamonds as well, the contract is impregnable, so East must defend on the assumption that West has that card. Even in the unlikely event that it is only doubleton, it will probably be enough. After winning the queen of diamonds with dummy's king and knocking out the ace of spades, declarer will surely finesse when another diamond is played by East.

It is not normal to lead the queen without holding the jack as well, but as B.J. Becker had Holmes saying, occasionally logic supersedes convention.

Playing with Edith in a Regional Swiss teams in Puerto Vallarta, I was once faced with a most curious situation.

Dlr: South   ♠ A K J
Vul: None   ♡ 6 3 2
                  ♢ A 10 7 3
                  ♣ A 8 5

♠ 9 7 6 5   ♠ 3 2
♡ J 10 9 4   ♡ 7 5
♢ Q 5 4 2   ♢ J 8 6
♣ J   ♣ Q 10 9 7 3 2

                  ♠ Q 10 8 4
                  ♡ A K Q 8
                  ♢ K 9
                  ♣ K 6 4

West	North	East	South
			1NT
Pass	6NT	Pass	Pass
Pass			

Sitting West, I made the obvious lead of the jack of hearts. Declarer won in hand, cashed four rounds of spades, two top clubs and his other heart winners to give this position:

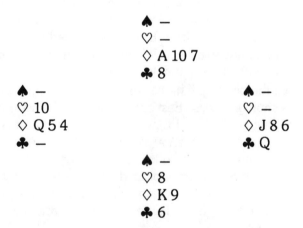

Now South had a choice of endplays. If he had decided to throw in Edith with a club, I would have discarded a diamond and Edith would have returned a *low* diamond as she had a count on declarer's hand. However, when South chose to give me a trick with the ten of hearts, Edith had to keep the queen of clubs and pitch a diamond. At this point I had to be careful to return a *low* diamond and Edith had to play low also, knowing that South had only a doubleton. Declarer was able to win the trick with the nine and cash the king, but he had to concede the last trick to Edith (or to me if he had chosen to overtake the king with dummy's ace).

If I had not been sure Edith would retain her jack of diamonds, I would have exited with the queen and hoped declarer would go wrong by winning with his king and finessing dummy's ten.

My Tip for a Top

When the defenders have the queen and jack in a suit and are forced to break it open, it is essential to try to determine whether either opposing hand contains only a doubleton, and to lead a high or low card accordingly. Generally, lead an *honor through length*, or *low through the (possible) doubleton*. With three cards each in the dummy and the concealed hand, lead the honor to give declarer a guess.

Chapter 21

The Exception that *Improves* the Rule

Man can improve himself but never will himself be perfect.

It's no use raising a Shout, *W.H. Auden*

A universally approved principle states that when you signal to partner that you like the suit he has led, you play the highest card you can spare (unless you are using upside-down signals, of course). This is especially true when you have cards in sequence. Thus, suppose partner leads the ten of hearts against a notrump contract, and this is what you can see:

Dummy
♡ A

You
♡ Q J 7

Drop the queen to promise the jack and deny the king.

Here is another possibility:

Dlr: South		♠ 8 4 2	
Vul: Both		♡ A	
		◇ K Q 5 4 3	
		♣ J 9 8 7	

♠ K J 5 3		♠ A 7 6
♡ K 7 6 4 2		♡ J 10 9 5
◇ 9 2		◇ J 10 7 6
♣ K 2		♣ 4 3

		♠ Q 10 9	
		♡ Q 8 3	
		◇ A 8	
		♣ A Q 10 6 5	

West	North	East	South
			1♣
Pass	1◇	Pass	1NT
Pass	2NT	Pass	3NT
Pass	Pass	Pass	

West leads the four of hearts. East should play the jack under the ace, which tells partner that South holds the queen. Declarer takes the club finesse, and when West wins with the king he knows he must try to get his partner on lead. Realizing that the ace of diamonds can wait if that is East's entry (declarer must have at most five club, one heart and two spade tricks), he switches to the five of spades, leading his higher spot because he wants a heart back, not a spade.

Now the spotlight falls on East. If he returns the nine of hearts (not the ten, which he is known to hold), the defenders must take at least four hearts, two spades and a club; and can cash four spades to defeat the contract by *five* tricks! However, if East plays back a spade, the contract will go two down, declarer losing one club, one heart and four spade tricks.

The same principle applies when you follow to a suit that declarer leads.

Dummy
♡ A 9

You
♡ J 10 8 7

If declarer leads the ace from the dummy, contribute your jack as the fall of the nine on the next round solidifies your sequence.

Dummy
♡ A J

You
♡ K Q 10 9

If declarer leads toward the dummy, put in the king to tell partner you have solid cards headed by the king-queen-ten. Without the ten, just insert the queen.

A similar rule governs the return lead from touching cards: play back the highest. However, there will occasionally be exceptional circumstances when partner will be able to read a false card because he will know declarer cannot have the card you are concealing.

A pretty example cropped up in the 1985 Caransa-Mai Swiss Teams, played in the Amsterdam Hilton.

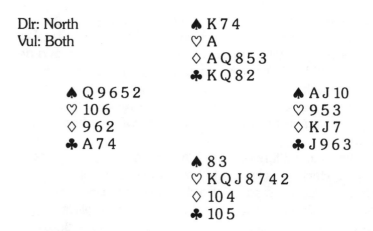

Dlr: North
Vul: Both

At both tables South played in four hearts, and both Wests led a low spade. When Michel Perron and Paul Chemla were sitting West and East, declarer put up dummy's king and East won with the ace. According to the textbooks, Chemla should have returned the jack of spades, but in fact he led back the ten. Perron, figuring that declarer would have played low from the dummy at trick one if he held the jack of spades, read the situation perfectly. He overtook the ten of spades with the queen and switched to a diamond, thus ensuring the defeat of the contract.

At the other table, East did not have the opportunity to make this "exception to the rule" play because the declarer, Philippe Soulet, saw the need to keep West off the lead, and so didn't put up dummy's king of spades at trick one. East won with the ten and returned a trump to dummy's ace. Soulet ensured East kept the lead by playing dummy's king of spades. East was able to exit with his third spade, but declarer ruffed, drew trumps, played a club to the king, and a club from the dummy. Luck was with Soulet when this left the defenders with no riposte. If East didn't go up with his jack, declarer's ten would force the ace, setting up dummy's queen for a diamond discard; and when East did win with the jack and played another club, declarer ruffed, bringing down the ace. (If it hadn't, declarer would have run his trumps for a show-up squeeze on West, assuming he had the ace of clubs and king of diamonds.)

A one-suited example of this type of play occurs in this situation:

Dummy

◇ K 8 7 6

West　　　　　　　　　　　　　East

◇ Q 5 2　　　　　　　　　　　◇ A 10 9

Declarer

◇ J 4 3

Needing to establish a diamond trick for his contract but not being able to afford three quick losers, declarer had reason to believe East had the ace, so he made the unusual play of leading the jack. However, when West covered with the queen, dummy's king was withheld. East dropped the nine. West knew that South didn't have the ten because he had not covered the queen with the king, so West continued with the five and East collected two more tricks. If East had played the ten on the first round, West might (incorrectly) have thought he held only a doubleton.

My Tip for a Top

When an exceptional play will make it easier for partner to read the situation, let the exception improve the rule.

Section C

Declarer-Play

The Prologue

The prologue is the grace,
Each act, a course, each scene, a different dish.

The Inconstant, *George Farquhar*

1. Dlr: South
Vul: Both

♠ A K 5
♡ K Q 2
◇ 7 4 2
♣ A J 9 4

♠ 9 7 3
♡ A J 3
◇ A K Q
♣ K 10 5 3

West	North	East	South
			1NT
Pass	6NT	Pass	Pass
Pass			

West leads the queen of spades. What is your line of play?

(Page 174)

2. Dlr: South
Vul: None

♠ 6 4 2
♡ 10 8 7
◇ A 10 9 6 5
♣ A 2

♠ A Q
♡ A 3 2
◇ K J 2
♣ Q J 8 7 5

West	North	East	South
			1NT
Pass	3NT	Pass	Pass
Pass			

West leads the jack of spades, East contributing the seven. How do you hope to collect nine tricks?

(Page 176)

3. Dlr: East   ♠ A Q 8 4
Vul: Both   ♡ 3
                                    ◇ A K J 7
                                    ♣ A 9 7 2
                                                        ♠ 6 5
                                                        ♡ K 10 9
                                                        ◇ Q 10 6 5
                                                        ♣ K 10 4 3

West	North	East	South
		Pass	Pass
3♡	Dble	Pass	4♠
Pass	Pass	Pass	

This hand is from a pair event. West leads the ace of hearts, then switches to the three of diamonds. Declarer wins with dummy's king, leads a trump to hand, ruffs a heart with the ace of spades, and plays a trump to his ten, West following. The nine of diamonds comes next, West discarding a heart, and dummy playing low.

In with the ten of diamonds, what do you do now?

(Page 161)

4. With neither side vulnerable, sitting West you pick up:

♠ J 5 4 3   ♡ Q J 10 9 8   ◇ 10 7   ♣ K 6

The bidding against you goes:

North	South
1♣	2♠
3♣	3♠
4♠	4NT (a)
5◇	5NT (a)
6◇	6♠
Pass	

(a) Simple Blackwood

What is your opening lead?

(Page 180)

5. Dlr: East   ♠ J 9 7 6 4
Vul: N-S   ♡ J 2
                  ◇ 8 5
                  ♣ Q J 4 3

                  ♠ A K
                  ♡ A Q 10 9 6 5 4
                  ◇ K 3
                  ♣ A 8

West	North	East	South
		1NT (a)	Dble
2◇	2♠	Pass	4♡ (b)
Pass	Pass	Pass	

(a) 10-12 points
(b) "I have game in my own hand."

The opening lead is the two of diamonds, fifth-best. East wins with the ace, and returns the three of hearts. How do you continue from here?

(Page 179)

6. Dlr: South   ♠ K 4 2
Vul: Both   ♡ J 10 7
                  ◇ Q 6 5 2
                  ♣ 9 6 5

                  ♠ Q 8 7 5
                  ♡ A Q
                  ◇ A K J 10 9 8 7
                  ♣ —

West	North	East	South
			1◇
Pass	1NT	2♣	3♣
4♣	4◇	5♣	5◇
Pass	Pass	Pass	

The opening lead is the two of clubs, East playing the king. What is your line of play?

(Page 183)

7. Dlr: South   ♠ 2
Vul: N-S   ♡ A 8 6 4
        ♢ A J 7 3
        ♣ A 9 8 2

        ♠ A K Q 9 8 6 5
        ♡ 5 2
        ♢ 4 2
        ♣ 7 5

West	North	East	South
			3♠
Pass	4♠	Pass	Pass
Pass			

West leads the king of hearts. Over to you.

(Page 184)

Chapter 1

Vanishing Tricks

But oh, beamish nephew, beware of the day,
If your Snark be a Boojum! For then
You will softly and suddenly vanish away,
And never be met with again!

The Baker's Tale, *Lewis Carroll*

I like magicians and illusionists; to see them perform in circuses and nightclubs has always been a favorite attraction for me. Among the many tricks and sleights of hand, one has always puzzled me. I saw it in Las Vegas. Two brothers made their lovely assistant disappear and substitute her with a wild animal, a lion or a tiger.

Magic at the bridge table is rare but by no means impossible. I'm not referring to the brilliant declarer who conjures tricks out of nowhere, or to the champion who surprises experienced Vu-Graph commentators with unexpected plays. Below you will see two plays in which one of declarer's losers disappears together with the defenders' "sure" winner.

You can find these plays categorized in textbooks under different names, but they are rare species in the bridge zoo. They are even more rare in real life at the table.

The first deal occurred during the Open Pairs at the 1978 Mexican Nationals.

Dlr: West   ♠ K 10 8 4
Vul: N-S   ♡ J 10 7 4 2
                     ◇ K 2
                     ♣ 4 3

♠ Q 5 3   ♠ J 6
♡ K 8 6 5   ♡ A Q 3
◇ Q 10 7   ◇ 9 8 4 3
♣ 10 9 8   ♣ Q 7 6 5

                     ♠ A 9 7 2
                     ♡ 9
                     ◇ A J 6 5
                     ♣ A K J 2

West	*North*		*East*	*South*	
Pass	Pass		Pass	1◇	
Pass	1♡		Pass	1♠	
Pass	2♠		Pass	3♣	
Pass	3◇		Pass	4NT	(a)
Pass	5◇	(b)	Pass	5♡	(c)
Pass	5♠	(d)	Pass	Pass	
Pass					

(a) Roman Key Card Blackwood
(b) One key card
(c) Asking for the queen of spades
(d) Denying her majesty

West led the ten of clubs. Perhaps North shouldn't have bid three diamonds, but five spades — one of the least aesthetic contracts — looked safe, with a loser in each major. But was it possible to make six?

The hand obviously called for a cross-ruff. Declarer won the first trick in hand and led his heart. East won with the queen and returned not the trump South was expecting, but a club.

Declarer won the club in hand, cashed the ace of diamonds, crossed to the king of diamonds, and ruffed a heart in hand. A diamond ruff, a heart ruff, and the last club winner left this position:

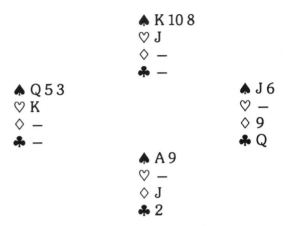

The play of the jack of diamonds left West with no answer. If he discarded, dummy's heart would be thrown. Then the two of clubs would kill the defenders' apparent trump trick. But when West ruffed low, dummy overruffed, and the jack of hearts was led. Now East was facing the frying-pan. If he discarded or ruffed low, South would win the trick with the nine of spades and have a high cross-ruff for the last two tricks. And when he ruffed with the jack of spades, declarer overruffed, then led the two of clubs. He had to score both the ten and king of spades for plus 680.

What happened to the defenders' sure trump trick? It vanished without trace. Devilish? Of course, and that's why this play is called the Devil's Coup.

True, an initial trump lead, which would sacrifice a trump trick, would probably hold declarer to eleven tricks; though twelve can be won. Work it out for yourself!

The second hand occurred during a club duplicate in Mexico City in 1988.

Dlr: North   ♠ K 8 6
Vul: N-S   ♡ Q J 3
                              ◇ A Q 5 3
                              ♣ A 8 7

♠ J 10 9 7 5   ♠ Q 2
♡ —   ♡ A 10 9 4
◇ K 9 8 6   ◇ J 10 7 2
♣ K Q 6 2   ♣ 10 9 3

                              ♠ A 4 3
                              ♡ K 8 7 6 5 2
                              ◇ 4
                              ♣ J 5 4

West	North	East	South
	1◇	Pass	1♡
Pass	1NT (a)	Pass	2♡
Pass	3♡	Pass	4♡
Pass	Pass	Pass	

(a) 12-16 points

North was supposed to pass over two hearts, but he liked his suitable maximum.

West led the jack of spades. There were four apparent losers, but after winning the first trick in hand and finessing the queen of diamonds successfully, the spade loser disappeared on the ace of diamonds.

Things had started well, but a bad trump break was still a possibility. Declarer ruffed a diamond in hand before leading a heart to the jack and ace. Back came a spade. Declarer won with dummy's king, and ruffed the eight of spades in hand, East discarding a club. This was the end-position:

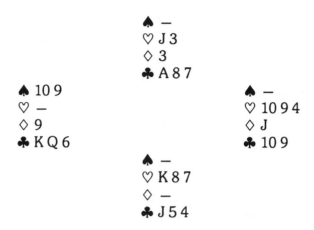

♠ —
♡ J 3
♢ 3
♣ A 8 7

♠ 10 9
♡ —
♢ 9
♣ K Q 6

♠ —
♡ 10 9 4
♢ J
♣ 10 9

♠ —
♡ K 8 7
♢ —
♣ J 5 4

A club to the ace and a diamond ruff brought declarer's tricks up to eight, and he still had two trump tricks to come. West's club winner and East's master trump both took trick thirteen.

If East returns a club rather than a spade at trick six, declarer wins in the dummy, ruffs a diamond, crosses to the king of spades, and leads the eight of spades. Whether East ruffs high or discards, declarer still gets ten tricks.

If the opening lead is the king of clubs, declarer ducks, wins the obligatory switch and proceeds as above. Though, funnily enough, declarer can even win trick one with the ace of clubs! He enters hand with a spade to the ace, finesses the queen of diamonds, and discards a club on the ace of diamonds. In this case, eventually West's spade winner is telescoped with East's trump winner.

Finally, what happens if East doesn't win the first trump trick? Declarer ruffs dummy's last diamond, plays a spade to the king, and leads the last spade. The ace of clubs and two trump tricks add up to ten.

What is the name of this play? It depends whether you look at it from declarer's point of view or from the perspective of the defense.

In the former case, it is a "trump elopement." You bring in your trump winners — in a way similar to the "coup en passant" — before the defenders can cash their winners.

In the latter case, it is a "compression play." The defenders' winners are compressed, or telescoped, together, falling upon each other. According to Phillip Alder, in Europe this play is sometimes called the "Concertina Coup," an hexagonal accordion-type musical instrument.

Modesty forbids my telling you who declared these two hands!

My Tip for a Top

If making your contract seems impossible, don't give up:

The opponents may make a mistake.

Some hands play themselves because the cards are luckily placed.

There may be a rare coup in the offing, which makes the defenders' sure trick(s) vanish — and you don't have to do it with mirrors!

Chapter 2

Strange Fascination

I have a left shoulder-blade that is a miracle of loveliness. People come miles to see it. My right elbow has a fascination that few can resist.

The Mikado, *W.S. Gilbert*

Often I wonder why advancing players are so fascinated by one particular aspect of declarer-play: the squeeze. Their attention seems to be excessively focussed on this infrequently occurring play, rather than on more mundane but extremely important topics like counting, card placement and probabilities.

Could this be interpreted as the surfacing of primitive atavistic instincts of violence, as some psychologists propose? Maybe the reason can be found in the title of the erudite opus of John L. Donelly, *Happiness is a Squeeze*.

Incidentally, do you know that the use of the term "squeeze" in bridge is of relatively recent vintage? The immortal Sidney Lenz adopted it during the 1920s from the "Squeeze Play" in baseball, and used it to replace the expression "forced discard" that was in vogue during those days.

For many bridge enthusiasts the mechanics of a squeeze are clouded in mystery, in spite of the numerous excellent texts by Coffin, Kelsey, Love and Reese, to name but a few.

Among the host of different squeezes, there are two which seem to offer even more difficulties than the others: the crisscross and trump squeezes.

These two are intimately related and are characterized by an apparent blockage in a "menace" suit. In addition, in the trump squeeze there is one trump left after the squeeze has taken place.

It is not my purpose in this chapter to delve deeply into the mechanics of these plays, nor to discuss the varied terminology used in the literature. (The terms I will use are those proposed by Hugh Kelsey.) Instead, I wish to describe two trump squeezes and use them to highlight the planning and execution necessary for success.

The first came up in a weekly duplicate game, with my wife, Edith, sitting South and cast in the role of the heroine.

Dlr: North
Vul: None

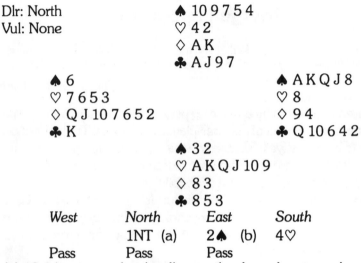

	West	North	East	South
		1NT (a)	2♠ (b)	4♡
	Pass	Pass	Pass	

(a) 12-14 points — but hardly a textbook weak notrump!
(b) Spades and clubs

West led a spade, and East played three rounds of the suit, declarer ruffing the last. West discarded two diamonds.

Edith played all her trumps except one. Next she led a club and ducked when West's king appeared. West had to return a diamond, and this four-card end-position resulted:

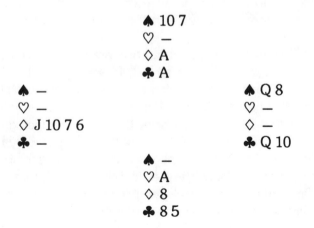

The lead of the ace of diamonds brought the trump squeeze to its climax. East could not make a winning discard and Edith had to collect the rest of the tricks.

Notice that it would not help West to discard his singleton king of clubs on the second round of spades and to ruff East's club switch. The count would have been rectified for the trump squeeze and it would operate in the same way.

My second example came up during the 1988 Mexican Open Pairs Championship.

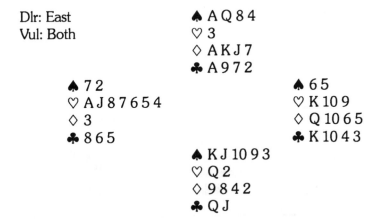

Dlr: East
Vul: Both

♠ A Q 8 4
♡ 3
◇ A K J 7
♣ A 9 7 2

♠ 7 2
♡ A J 8 7 6 5 4
◇ 3
♣ 8 6 5

♠ 6 5
♡ K 10 9
◇ Q 10 6 5
♣ K 10 4 3

♠ K J 10 9 3
♡ Q 2
◇ 9 8 4 2
♣ Q J

The bidding was similar at most tables. After two passes, West opened three hearts, North doubled, and South bid four spades.

The first six tricks were essentially identical at all tables. The ace of hearts was led, followed by a switch to the three of diamonds. Declarer won in the dummy with the king, led a trump to hand, ruffed his last heart with the ace of spades, and played a trump to the ten. The nine of diamonds followed and, when West discarded a heart, it was run to East's ten.

At this point practically all the Easts missed the winning defense to hold South to ten tricks, suffering from a blind spot — or should I say an optical illusion?

Not realizing that a diamond or heart return would not give declarer an extra trick and would guarantee a trick for the king of clubs, every East returned a low club. (Switching to the *king* of clubs would be better than leading a low one. Not only does it break up the trump squeeze, but also it allows for South's having jack doubleton of clubs; though, it is true, that would make his four-spade bid excessive.)

Now declarer could win with the queen of clubs and cash one round of trumps to give this position:

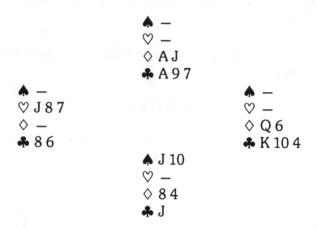

```
                        ♠ —
                        ♡ —
                        ◇ A J
                        ♣ A 9 7
♠ —                                          ♠ —
♡ J 8 7                                      ♡ —
◇ —                                          ◇ Q 6
♣ 8 6                                        ♣ K 10 4
                        ♠ J 10
                        ♡ —
                        ◇ 8 4
                        ♣ J
```

On the penultimate trump, dummy releases the jack of diamonds and East is caught in a trump squeeze.

Unfortunately, none of the declarers found this play.

My Tip for a Top

When you are one trick short of your contract and no endplay seems possible, think of the trump squeeze.

Remember the necessary conditions for this play:

All but one of the trumps have been played.

Dummy holds a singleton master card in one suit, two low cards in the other menace suit and another entry card.

Try to visualize the end-position and plan the play accordingly.

Declarer has a void in dummy's two-card-menace suit, one trump, which serves as a ruffing entry, and two low cards (a split menace) in the blocked suit. (Note, though, that in the above hand dummy has a three-card-menace suit and declarer a singleton, rather than two cards opposite a void.)

Chapter 3

The Enemy is Your Friend

He [George Bernard Shaw] hasn't an enemy in the world, and none of
his friends like him.

Oscar Wilde

Let's face it, we all like to be declarer, putting utter faith in our
abilities to surmount the difficulties of tricky contracts. Being
red-blooded competitors, our egos echo the lyrics of a popular tune
of the past: "Anything you can do, I can do better."

Alas, often we encounter contracts that offer a multitude of
possible lines of play, but the path is narrow and there is only one
winning alternative. Don't despair! Even if you make the wrong
guess, all might not be lost: the opponents, lacking clairvoyance,
may not find the perfect defense.

Playing with my wife, Edith, in a barometer game in our club,
the following interesting hand cropped up, providing a good example of this.

Dlr: South	♠ J 9 6 3		
Vul: None	♡ Q 9 3		
	◇ K 10 8		
	♣ 8 4 3		

♠ Q 8 7 2		♠ 10
♡ 8		♡ K J 10 7 5 4
◇ J 7 4 2		◇ Q 6 5 3
♣ Q 10 7 6		♣ 5 2

	♠ A K 5 4	
	♡ A 6 2	
	◇ A 9	
	♣ A K J 9	

West	North		East	South
	E.R.			G.R.
				2♣
Pass	2◇	(a)	2♡	2NT (b)
Pass	3♣	(c)	Pass	3♠
Pass	4♠		Pass	Pass
Pass				

(a) Fewer than two controls
(b) 23-24 points
(c) Stayman

East was an aggressive player who believed in getting into the auction on any excuse, so when the opening lead of the eight of hearts was made, I was not sure whether it was from a doubleton or was a singleton. Therefore, when dummy's nine of hearts was covered by East's ten, I ducked, hoping that even if I had guessed wrongly, I could recover later.

East returned the seven of hearts, I played the six and West ruffed with the two of spades. But now he was faced with a dilemma. It appeared that a black-suit switch would present me with a trick, so, by a process of elimination, he returned the two of diamonds. East played the queen and I won with the ace. The king of spades brought down the seven from West and the ten from East. Now the East-West hands were pretty much an open book. It looked like East had started with 1-6-4-2 distribution and West with 4-1-4-4. A second high spade from hand seemed to confirm the diagnosis, East discarding a low heart.

Now came the burning question: Which minor-suit finesse to take? With apparent odds of 4-to-2 against the club finesse, the nine of diamonds was led to dummy's ten, which held. Next, the king of diamonds was cashed and the closed hand discarded the nine of clubs. Declarer played a heart to the ace, and West elected to discard the six of clubs. The ace of clubs was cashed, and a spade led to endplay West. He had the unappetizing choice between leading a club into my tenace and giving a ruff-and-discard with the last diamond, allowing me to get rid of my losing club. The contract was made for a top.

Did the opponents find the best defense? Definitely not! Looking at dummy's diamond holding, West should allow for the possibility that East has the queen and South the doubleton ace. As I pointed out in *No Rules are Cast in Iron* (page 136), the winning return in these situations is the *honor* from H x x (x) and *not* a low card, in order to prevent a subsequent winning finesse. At trick three, West should return the *jack* of diamonds.

I leave it to the analytically-minded reader to decide whether the contract can be made if East does not return a heart, but switches to a low diamond at trick two; or, for that matter, to any other card.

Strangely enough, double-dummy the contract can always be made if declarer wins the first trick with the ace of hearts. He cashes the ace of spades, noting the drop of the ten, and eliminates the diamonds. Next, he plays three rounds of clubs, giving rise to this end-position with West on lead:

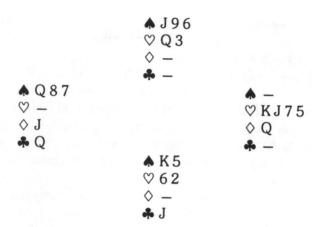

A spade or diamond return would hand declarer his tenth trick, so West has to lead the queen of clubs. But to no avail: Declarer ruffs in the dummy and exits with a heart, East winning. With only trumps left, poor West has to ruff the next trick and lead away from the queen of trumps, giving South his contract.

My Tip for a Top

Whenever possible, know your opponents. Familiarize yourself with their style of bidding and play. It will often help you to make the right guess.

If you have picked the wrong line from many alternatives, don't give up. They might be having as much trouble in selecting the winning defense. Perfect defenders are rare: *Errare humanum est.*

Chapter 4

With a Little Bit of Luck

Back of the bar, in a solo game, sat Dangerous Dan McGrew,
And watching his luck was his light-o'-love, the lady that's known as Lou.

The Shooting of Dan McGrew, *Robert W. Service*

Sometimes every red-blooded bridge player finds himself in a deplorable contract. The reactions that follow will mirror with great precision the character of the actor involved. Some start berating their partners for their imbecile bidding; others silently bemoan their fate in having to put up with supreme incompetency; rarely they start blaming themselves for gross errors; but only a few set out to do the reasonable thing: to make the best out of a bad situation.

Occasionally the gods of bridge reward you for good behavior and place the cards favorably. So you roll up your sleeves, go about your work and hope for the best!

At the 1990 World Olympiad in Geneva, Miguel Reygadas and I got in a mess when holding the following collection of cards:

Dlr: South   ♠ A Q J 9 6 3
Vul: E-W   ♡ 2
                              ◇ A Q 10
                              ♣ K 3 2

                              ♠ K 10
                              ♡ A Q 7 5 4
                              ◇ 7 2
                              ♣ J 10 9 4

West	North	East	South
	Reygadas		*Rosenkranz*
			1♡ (a)
Pass	2NT (b)	Pass	3♠ (c)
Pass	4NT (d)	Pass	5♡ (e)
Pass	6♠	Pass	Pass
Pass			

(a) A little light, to say the least!
(b) A jump shift in spades
(c) A top honor in spades
(d) Roman Key Card Blackwood
(e) Two key cards but no queen of spades

When dummy hit the table I said to myself that it served me right for making such a feather-light opening bid. But what's done is done and I went about my business.

The opening lead was the ace of clubs, East encouraging with the five (their card was marked upside-down count and attitude). I tried to muddy the waters by false-carding with the nine, but this play had no effect on my champion LHO, who without hesitation continued with the seven of clubs.

Starting out with nine sure tricks for a slam, I began the search for three more. I assumed that the queen of clubs was on my right. West probably would not have led the ace from the ace-queen. Therefore somehow I had to get rid of dummy's third club. The only possibility was to lead dummy's heart singleton and pray that the king of hearts was *chez* East. When East followed with the three of hearts, I closed my eyes and put in the queen. When I opened them again, I saw West's jack resting on the table. Great, but my troubles were yet not over. I cashed the ace of hearts, discarding dummy's club loser, then I had to take the diamond finesse and, when it succeeded, play the ace of diamonds and ruff a diamond in my hand.

Luck was with me, and everything went as I hoped. After ruffing dummy's last diamond in hand, I cashed the king of spades, entered dummy by ruffing a third heart with an honor, drew the outstanding trumps, and apologized to my opponents for the undeserved top (the results were scored over the field!).

West's wry remark was: "I'm surprised you didn't bid six notrump. Miguel would have made it as the double finesse in diamonds also works!"

This was the complete deal:

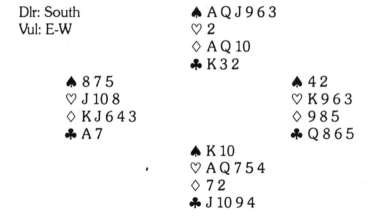

Dlr: South
Vul: E-W

♠ A Q J 9 6 3
♡ 2
◊ A Q 10
♣ K 3 2

♠ 8 7 5
♡ J 10 8
◊ K J 6 4 3
♣ A 7

♠ 4 2
♡ K 9 6 3
◊ 9 8 5
♣ Q 8 6 5

♠ K 10
♡ A Q 7 5 4
◊ 7 2
♣ J 10 9 4

The moral of the story is, as Clarence Darrow said: "There is no such thing as justice — in and out of court." And I can add: "Or at the bridge table."

My Tip for a Top

Even if you have reached a hopeless contract, don't give up. Think of a lie of cards that will allow you to fulfill your contract; or, when defending, to defeat the opponents.

Be an optimist, luck may be with you!

Chapter 5

Render unto Caesar

Upon what meat doth this our Caesar feed,
That he is grown so great?

Julius Caesar, *William Shakespeare*

Thumbing for the umpteenth time through Clyde Love's masterpiece, *Bridge Squeezes Complete*, I was impressed by this sentence: "The difference between an expert and a dub is roughly this: Playing three notrump, the expert loses four tricks early, the dub loses five tricks late."

Recognizing the importance of the basic rule, "Lose your sure losers early," and being impressed by Love's opinion that, "There are some millions of players whose game would greatly improve if they would assimilate this one fact," I decided to embark upon a minor research project, to classify the bridge situations where this tenet can be applied profitably.

Here are the results of my quest, which yielded ten situations. I am sure that careful analysis will come up with more, where losing a trick early is mandatory. However, here is my selection, the first being in Love's honor:

1. To Rectify the Count for a Squeeze
No examples are needed as textbooks are full of them.

2. The Holdup by Declarer
Again, examples galore can be found in the literature. But here are two simple positions. The first is the classic Bath Coup:

Dummy
♠ 7 6 2

LHO
♠ K led

Declarer
♠ A J 4

Declarer ducks when the king is led. If West continues the suit, the declarer collects two tricks. If West switches, declarer still has the suit under control.

This situation is often misplayed when RHO, not LHO, rates to get the lead:

Dummy

♠ 5 4 2

LHO   *RHO*

♠ A 10 8 7 3   ♠ Q 9

Declarer

♠ K J 6

LHO leads a low card against a notrump contract, and RHO puts up the queen.

Thousands of players pounce thoughtlessly upon the queen, to regret it later when RHO gains the lead and returns the suit through the king. A duck on the first round would turn the contract from no-play into ironclad.

3. To Thwart a Holdup by the Defenders

Typically, when holding a low doubleton opposite K Q 10 9 x and needing only three tricks from the suit but being short of entries to the long suit, it is right to start by finessing the ten. If you lead low to the king, the next player will duck when holding A J x.

4. To Maintain Control

Often in trump contracts with a 4-4 or 4-3 fit, it is necessary to give up a trump trick early.

5. To Keep Your Communications Open

When you are faced with entry problems, or are in danger of blocking a source of winners in a long suit, duck a trick early. For example, with ace-third opposite king-fifth, give up the first trick (or the second after cashing the ace, the honor in the short side first).

6. To Sever the Opponents' Communications

Look up the Scissors Coup in a textbook on play.

7. To Protect a Useful High Card from being Ruffed

A typical scenario is that LHO has opened with a preempt and leads the king of his suit against your suit contract. You find ace-fourth or -fifth in dummy opposite your singleton. Duck the first trick, just in case RHO is void, and ruff the continuation in hand. Thus you will be able to use your ace later for an important discard.

8. To Foil the Opponents' Signals

The following hand from the 1989 Mexico City Spring Sectional provides a good example:

```
Dlr: East                    ♠ K 7 3 2
Vul: E-W                     ♡ A K 8 3
                             ◇ 10 9
                             ♣ 7 5 3
        ♠ 5 4                                      ♠ Q J 10
        ♡ J 10 9                                   ♡ Q 6 5
        ◇ A Q 7 4                                  ◇ J 8 6 5 2
        ♣ 8 6 4 2                                  ♣ J 10
                             ♠ A 9 8 6
                             ♡ 7 4 2
                             ◇ K 3
                             ♣ A K Q 9
```

West	North	East	South
		Pass	1NT
Pass	2♣	Pass	2♠
Pass	4♠	Pass	Pass
Pass			

Declarer considered ducking the opening lead of the jack of hearts, but fearing that East would overtake and shift to a diamond, he won in the dummy and immediately led the three of spades. East played the queen of spades and remained on lead, though declarer had hoped to duck the trick to West.

With no clear clues to go by, East made the wrong choice and returned the jack of clubs. Escaping the deadly diamond return through his king, declarer won with the ace of clubs, drew trumps, and was able to discard a losing diamond from dummy on the fourth round of clubs. Thus he lost only three tricks, one spade, one heart and one diamond, and made his contract. If declarer had played three rounds of spades, West would have discouraged in clubs to guide his partner's defense. Or do you think East missed an importance inference anyway?

9. To Avoid Allowing the Dangerous Opponent to Gain the Lead

Dorothy Truscott suggested the following teaching hand, which combines several important points:

```
Dlr: South          ♠ Q 6 4
Vul: E-W            ♡ 8 5 3
                   ◇ A 7
                   ♣ K 9 5 3 2
      ♠ 3 2                      ♠ 7 5
      ♡ A 10 9 2                 ♡ Q J 4
      ◇ K Q 9 8 5                ◇ J 10 6 4 2
      ♣ 7 6                      ♣ Q J 10
                   ♠ A K J 10 9 8
                   ♡ K 7 6
                   ◇ 3
                   ♣ A 8 4
```

West	North	East	South
			1♠
Pass	1NT	Pass	2♠
Pass	3♠	Pass	4♠
Pass	Pass	Pass	

The opening lead was the king of diamonds. Declarer *ducked* and East played the jack. The diamond continuation was won in the dummy, the four of clubs being discarded from the closed hand. Two rounds of trumps cleared the suit, and dummy's clubs were established with one ruff. There were two long cards available to provide two heart discards. Making eleven tricks instead of going one down if declarer had won the first trick!

10. To Lose a Trick to get the Count

I always admired the late Lew Mathe's dummy-play. He believed in taking extreme risks, even in trump contracts, by ducking early in order to get a count of the hand. Here is an example of his technique. It occurred during a Vanderbilt in the 60s.

Dlr: South   ♠ A K 5
Vul: Both   ♡ K Q 2
                        ◇ 7 4 2
                        ♣ A J 9 4

♠ Q J 10 8 6   ♠ 4 2
♡ 9 5   ♡ 10 8 7 6 4
◇ 6 5   ◇ J 10 9 8 3
♣ Q 8 6 2   ♣ 7

                        ♠ 9 7 3
                        ♡ A J 3
                        ◇ A K Q
                        ♣ K 10 5 3

West	North	East	South
			1NT
Pass	6NT	Pass	Pass
Pass			

After the opening lead of the queen of spades, the declarer had ten top tricks and had to guess the position of the queen of clubs for two additional tricks. The mirror distribution was annoying, but Mathe played the whole hand in barely two minutes. With no squeeze or endplay possible, he ducked the opening lead and won the spade continuation. Paying no attention to the opponents' signals, Mathe cashed the other top spade and six red-suit winners. When West discarded on the third round of both red suits and East on the third round of spades, the whole hand had counted out. Mathe cashed the king of clubs and claimed. He led the ten of clubs and finessed through West.

My Tip for a Top

If you must lose a trick in a suit, lose it early if you don't endanger your contract.

    Render therefore unto Caesar the things which are Caesar's.

Chapter 6

Don't Set Up the Trick that Beats You

His present and your pains we thank you for:
When we have match'd our rackets to these balls,
We will in France, by God's grace, play a set
Shall strike his father's crown into the hazard.

Henry V, *William Shakespeare*

It is interesting to observe how often even competent declarers suffer from "blind spots." My dear friend the late Dick Frey — one of the all-time greats — provided me with the following two hands from his weekly rubber-bridge game.

Dlr: North
Vul: None

♠ Q J 10 4 3
♡ K 2
◇ A K 10 9 5
♣ 10

♠ 9 2
♡ A Q 4
◇ J 6 3
♣ A J 8 4 2

North	South
1♠	2♣
2◇	2NT
3◇	3NT
Pass	

West led the five of hearts. Declarer won in his hand and, as one of the many addicts of "finessomania," immediately tried the diamond finesse, losing to East's queen. The grateful opponents eventually took two hearts and two spades in addition to their diamond trick, to set the ice cold contract. Instead of the futile diamond play, South should count his winners and realize that going after the spade suit will give him three spades, three hearts, two diamonds and a club for sure, before the heart suit is established. As a matter of fact, this line will yield eleven tricks if the queen of diamonds is singleton or doubleton.

This was the full deal:

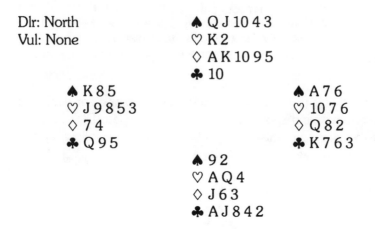

Dlr: North   ♠ Q J 10 4 3
Vul: None   ♡ K 2
       ◇ A K 10 9 5
       ♣ 10

♠ K 8 5   ♠ A 7 6
♡ J 9 8 5 3   ♡ 10 7 6
◇ 7 4   ◇ Q 8 2
♣ Q 9 5   ♣ K 7 6 3

     ♠ 9 2
     ♡ A Q 4
     ◇ J 6 3
     ♣ A J 8 4 2

The second example represents a slightly different situation.

Dlr: South   ♠ 6 4 2
Vul: None   ♡ 10 8 7
       ◇ A 10 9 6 5
       ♣ A 2

♠ K J 10 5 3   ♠ 9 8 7
♡ K J 5   ♡ Q 9 6 4
◇ 4 3   ◇ Q 8 7
♣ 10 6 3   ♣ K 9 4

     ♠ A Q
     ♡ A 3 2
     ◇ K J 2
     ♣ Q J 8 7 5

West	North	East	South
			1NT
Pass	3NT	Pass	Pass
Pass			

West led the jack of spades. This may appear to be an exception to the rule, but even if you take the diamond finesse the right way, you will still have only nine tricks; if it loses, you wind up one trick short. This is exactly what happened to our hasty declarer. A superior way to try for nine tricks is to tackle the club suit first by leading a low club to the ace and one back toward the queen-jack.

Whether or not the queen of clubs wins, you will make the contract if either the clubs split 3-3 or you guess correctly in diamonds. Also, you have the possibility of overtricks if the clubs are 3-3 and you drop a singleton or doubleton queen of diamonds.

My Tip for Top

Take your time to think about the hand.

Count your winners and losers.

If you can avoid it, don't set up the trick that may beat you.

Chapter 7

Dealing With Options

Nothing astonishes men so much as common-sense and plain dealing.

Essay on Art, *Ralph Waldo Emerson*

An interesting phenomenon has been the talk of the bridge world in recent years. A group of talented young experts, including two world champions, have positioned themselves as option traders in the principal US option exchanges, and have operated generally with great success, making millions of dollars in several instances.

This stellar performance hasn't even been marred by the big '87 October crash, when only a few excessive risk-takers suffered decisive setbacks.

The question often asked is: What is the key to the success story of these bridge experts: does their experience at the tables in some way relate to their accomplishments?

In my opinion it is the ability to make quick and reasoned decisions under stress, the same way as other professionals and executives have to act under critical conditions. Bridge is a good training ground for such activities.

At the bridge table we are dealing with a different kind of options, and here too these experts mentioned above have had ample experience. They are well versed in the art of creating, preserving and removing options.

Let me present to you an eloquent example, which occurred in my regular Monday evening duplicate game.

Dlr: East   ♠ J 9 7 6 4
Vul: N-S   ♡ J 2
                      ♢ 8 5
                      ♣ Q J 4 3

♠ 10 8 3 2   ♠ Q 5
♡ K   ♡ 8 7 3
♢ J 9 7 6 2   ♢ A Q 4 2
♣ 9 7 6   ♣ K 10 5 2

                       ♠ A K
                       ♡ A Q 10 9 6 5 4
                       ♢ K 3
                       ♣ A 8

West	*North*	*East*	*South*
Reygadas		*Rosenkranz*	
		1NT (a)	Dble
2♢	2♠	Pass	4♡ (b)
Pass	Pass	Pass	

(a) 10-12 points
(b) "I have game in my own hand."

The opening lead was the two of diamonds, fifth-best in our methods, and I won with the ace while South contributed the three. Trying to count declarer's hand, I reasoned: "South for his bidding surely holds at least seven hearts and, assuming my partner's bid wasn't psychic, he has two diamonds. Also, South most likely has the top cards in the black suits, and his distribution seems to be 2-7-2-2. My partner has at most a singleton heart, which may be the king.

"Declarer has no entry to the dummy to take a finesse in clubs or hearts, so he probably will have to lay down the ace of hearts when he gains the lead, felling Miguel's stiff king. Then the jack of hearts will become an entry to the dummy and he will finesse my king of clubs for twelve tricks and a top. Of course, he may try to lead a low heart toward dummy, but I doubt it."

I decided to offer him an option and returned the three of hearts. Delighted at having gained an unexpected entry to a seemingly unreachable dummy, and suddenly having the opportunity to try both finesses, one of which he knew must succeed after my opening bid, declarer played a low heart. West took his singleton king and, although declarer eventually finessed my king of clubs and collected eleven tricks, we earned an above-average score.

Was this another case of bewaring Greeks bearing gifts? You be the judge!

My policy in most of these cases is to take a good look at the quality of my opponent and, if he is a good player, to decline the option offered. At most of the tables this option will not arise, so I play with the field.

One of my favorite hands dealing with the removal of options is close to 30 years old, and was reported by Alfred Sheinwold. It describes a lead problem the late Lee Hazen solved, robbing declarer of one of his two vital options.

Hazen was West, holding

♠ J 5 4 3   ♡ Q J 10 9 8   ◇ 10 7   ♣ K 6

The bidding against him was:

North	South
1♣	2♠
3♣	3♠
4♠	4NT (a)
5◇	5NT (a)
6◇	6♠
Pass	

(a) Simple Blackwood

Sheinwold wrote: "No bell rang to tell Lee that he had to pick an unusual lead: nobody handed him the hand on a piece of paper. Nevertheless he came up with the killing lead — the six of clubs.

"The effect of this lead was exactly what Hazen had expected.

Dlr: South
Vul: None

```
                    ♠ 10 9 2
                    ♡ K 6
                    ◇ J 6
                    ♣ A Q J 9 7 4
    ♠ J 5 4 3                       ♠ —
    ♡ Q J 10 9 8                    ♡ 7 4 3 2
    ◇ 10 7                          ◇ Q 9 8 5 4 2
    ♣ K 6                           ♣ 10 5 3
                    ♠ A K Q 8 7 6
                    ♡ A 5
                    ◇ A K 3
                    ♣ 8 2
```

"Declarer was foolish enough to think that his trump suit was solid. He could afford to lose one club trick, but he did not want to expose himself to a club ruff. So he went up with the ace of clubs — for down one. If Hazen had led any other suit, declarer would have found out about the losing trump. Then he would have had to take the club finesse, making the slam."

My Tip for a Top

As a defender, look out for the opportunity to create a losing option for declarer.

As a declarer, be careful with new options offered to you, unless you can preserve your original chances in addition to the new one.

Chapter 8

Flying Fingers = Futile Plans

Sed fugit interea, fugit inreparabile tempus.

But meanwhile it is flying, irretrievable time is flying.

Virgil

Planning is the buzzword of our decade. Terms like program, scheme and forecast have found their way into our daily vocabulary. Maybe it all started with the Marshall Plan, but nowadays governments have their five-year plans for economic growth; companies issue stock option plans, savings plans and health care plans for their employees. Athletes follow a blueprint for their training. Airlines are showering us with plans for frequent fliers; and most of us in our private lives are planning our daily activities, our careers, the education of our children, our vacations and, of course, our retirement. Hardly anything is left for improvisation.

In bridge, one of the first things we are taught is to pause after the opening lead has been made and the dummy tabled. The idea is to take time to form a game plan.

Sounds simple, doesn't it? Yet when it comes to implementing this sage advice, what do we find? An almost irresistible impulse to get going and make that play to the first trick quickly, often confident in the accumulated experience of thousands of hands in our subconscious mind.

True, the average player sins in this respect more often than the seasoned expert, but even at the highest levels we encounter the peccadillo of impetuous action.

Let me show you two examples from a Sectional tournament in Palo Alto. Both were misplayed at most tables in the heat of the competition. Both share one feature: the proper care of entries.

Dlr: South
Vul: Both

	♠ K 4 2	
	♡ J 10 7	
	◇ Q 6 5 2	
	♣ 9 6 5	

♠ J 10 9 6		♠ A 3
♡ K 9 6 2		♡ 8 5 4 3
◇ 4 3		◇ —
♣ Q 4 2		♣ A K J 10 8 7 3

	♠ Q 8 7 5	
	♡ A Q	
	◇ A K J 10 9 8 7	
	♣ —	

West	North	East	South
			1◇
Pass	1NT	2♣	3♣
4♣	4◇	5♣	5◇
Pass	Pass	Pass	

The opening lead was the two of clubs. Declarer has two probable spade losers and a heart loser if the finesse fails.

One line, popular in Palo Alto, was to draw trumps and try the heart finesse.

An additional possibility can be envisioned in the spade suit. If the ace is doubleton, two tricks can be scored by guessing who has the ace. In this case, the bidding points to East as the owner of this card. Also, his club length makes it more likely to find him with spade shortness.

Which play to make first: the spade lead from dummy or the heart finesse?

If there were sufficient entries to the dummy, it would not make any difference. However, here the diamond suit provides only one immediate entry to dummy. Therefore, declarer's plan, after going through this somewhat lengthy thought process, should be to ruff the club lead in hand, draw two rounds of trumps ending in the dummy, and play a spade to the queen. If the queen of spades holds, lead a second spade and play low from the dummy. If East has to win with the ace, all is well. If not, after losing two spades, declarer's final spade (even if now high!) is ruffed in the dummy. This provides a late second entry and permits the heart finesse to be attempted.

As the cards lie, the heart finesse loses but the spade play works. However, most impatient declarers went down in this excellent five-diamond contract by trying the heart finesse first. It lost, and suddenly they realized they did not have a reentry to the dummy for the spade play.

The second example requires even more foresight.

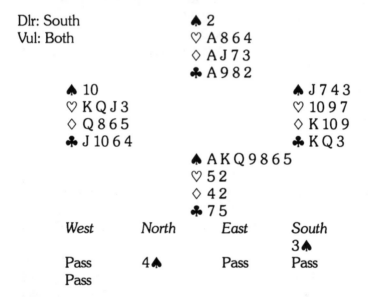

```
Dlr: South              ♠ 2
Vul: Both               ♡ A 8 6 4
                        ◇ A J 7 3
                        ♣ A 9 8 2
        ♠ 10                         ♠ J 7 4 3
        ♡ K Q J 3                    ♡ 10 9 7
        ◇ Q 8 6 5                    ◇ K 10 9
        ♣ J 10 6 4                   ♣ K Q 3
                        ♠ A K Q 9 8 6 5
                        ♡ 5 2
                        ◇ 4 2
                        ♣ 7 5

        West        North        East        South
                                              3♠
        Pass        4♠           Pass         Pass
        Pass
```

The opening lead was the king of hearts. If the trumps break, there are ten easy tricks: seven spades and three aces. But a good declarer always asks himself what could go wrong. If the trumps are 5-0 or 4-1, with West having the length, nothing can be done. But if East has four spades and West holds the singleton ten or jack, the contract may be makable with a trump coup. However, it takes careful planning. South must shorten himself by ruffing three times in his hand, leaving himself with the same number of trumps as his RHO. For the three ruffs, he needs three entries to the dummy; and he has to retain an exit card to play at trick eleven. In other words, he has to plan the play at trick one, visualizing the position ten tricks later! Quite a task which requires a lot of hard work.

This is how the play proceeds: Duck the opening lead, win the heart continuation and make the key play of ruffing a heart in hand at trick three. (True, this takes a slight risk that West has led from a doubleton heart and spades were 3-2 all along, but at the time table presence suggested this was not the case.) Two high trumps reveal the unfavorable break but, when West shows up with the singleton ten of spades, declarer proceeds as planned. A minor suit is ducked, the second round won in the dummy, and a third round of the suit is ruffed in hand. The other minor-suit ace provides the entry for the last heart ruff. Declarer has the queen-nine of spades and a losing minor-suit card left. He exits with the minor-suit card to catch East in a trump coup. *Voilà*, and well done!

If, after ducking in one minor, the defenders switch to the second minor, you take the heart ruff at that point, return to dummy in the ducked minor, take a ruff in that suit, and exit for the coup.

As expected, few declarers found the winning line.

My Tip for a Top

Think of the two Ps: *pause* and *plan* at trick one.
  Take good care of your entries.
  Be an optimist, but prepare for the worst.

Section D

General

Chapter 1

How to Achieve Good Results with an Unfamiliar Partner

At night returning, every labour sped,
He sits down the monarch of a shed;
Smiles by his cheerful fire, and round surveys
His children's looks, that brighten at the blaze;
While his lov'd partner, boastful of her hoard,
Displays her cleanly platter on the board.

The Traveller, *Oliver Goldsmith*

Looking back over the past years, what is your record of playing for the first time with new partners? Maybe it parallels mine. Partnered for the first time by leading experts like Bobby Jordan, Ivar Stakgold and Norman Kay, we came up with scores in excess of 64 percent in two-session games, and we had zero misunderstandings. Maybe you will argue that the outstanding quality of these partners invalidates the significance of these excellent scores. But then on a different level in club games I had similar good performances in first-time partnerships. Is there a secret to these results?

One of my expert friends who shares with me this type of experience observes cynically: "The first time there is mutual respect and caution, each going out of his way to make it easy on partner. The second time you become a little bit relaxed. The third time everybody is on his own: 'Familiarity breeds misunderstandings'."

I agree with this to a certain extent, but I attribute success in new partnerships to these ideas:

1. Use the time available for discussion and agreement on essentials.

2. Let your partner select the basic system but make it as simple as possible.

3. Don't insist on your pet ideas.

4. Define what is forcing, invitational, sign-off.

5. Keep artificial bids and conventions to a minimum.

6. Four notrump should be always Blackwood, not quantitative or obscurely unusual.

7. Doubles are for take-out, negative or penalty. Avoid conventional expert doubles (game-try, maximum-overcall or Rosenkranz).

8. Forcing passes and cue-bids must be completely obvious even to a kibitzer.

9. Keep bidding and defensive signaling simple and clear.

10. Make a general rule about ambiguous undiscussed bids: Either all forcing or all non-forcing, whichever is your preference.

11. Don't make "Master Bids" — save them for your regular partner.

12. If you are not sure of any bid, select the one which is likely to cost the least if you are wrong.

I have selected four hands to illustrate my points. The first is one of the most widely-publicized bidding misunderstandings in bridge history.

	♠ Q		♠ K J 4 3
	♡ K Q J 8 3		♡ 10 9 7 2
	◇ Q		◇ J 9 7 6 2
	♣ K Q J 10 9 3		♣ —
	Opener		*Responder*
	1♣		1◇
	1♡		3♡
	4NT (a)		5♣
	7♡!	(Dble)	Pass
	Pass		

(a) Simple Blackwood

The deal occurred in the last round of the qualifying section of the 1971 Bermuda Bowl in Taipei. The French had already reached the semifinals, so the non-playing captain split two of his pairs, putting in two players who had no history as partners.

The problem came from the interpretation of the three-heart

bid. The responder thought it was a limit raise, but the opener took it as strong and forcing. When the opener launched into Blackwood and heard the five-club reply, he "knew" his partner couldn't have zero aces for his forcing bid. He was happy to bid seven hearts. North's double suggested that something had gone wrong.

Regardless of the meaning for three hearts, the opener shouldn't have bid seven hearts. He should have "signed off" in five hearts. If his partner had four aces, he wouldn't pass. This is a standard treatment for any ambiguous Blackwood sequence. True, five hearts is one too high, but minus 50 (it was unlikely to be doubled) would have been less expensive than minus 500.

In the other room, they bid 1♥-2♥-4♥-Pass for plus 420 and fourteen imps.

My second hand comes from a side game at the Nationals in Winnipeg, where two excellent players were practicing for a Swiss Team event. It revolves around the use of a four-notrump bid. It reminds me of an anecdote. (There is no guarantee of the veracity of the story as my information is not first-hand!) Marshall Miles, opening his explanation of four-notrump bids, began: "Not all four-notrump bids are Blackwood." Thereupon half of his class stood up and walked out.

♠ 8	♠ A Q 10 9 5
♡ Q J 4	♡ A K 6 3
◇ A K Q J 10 7 6	◇ 4 2
♣ K 4	♣ A Q
Opener	*Responder*
1◇	1♠
3NT	4NT
Pass	

As you can see, there are fourteen top tricks for the taking, yet our friends played in the embarrassing contract of four notrump. I leave it to you to judge who was wrong: West for passing or East for bidding four notrump rather than another, unambiguous bid.

The third hand is taken from a Swiss Team event during the 1986 Mexican Nationals, where I watched two highly-ranked players from different ends of the country have a misunderstanding.

```
Dlr: South              ♠ Q 9 3 2
Vul: Both               ♡ J 6 2
                        ◊ A 7 6 4
                        ♣ 4 3
        ♠ J 10 8                        ♠ 6
        ♡ A K 10 9 4                    ♡ Q 8 5 3
        ◊ Q 10                          ◊ J 8 3
        ♣ Q 9 8                         ♣ K J 7 6 5
                        ♠ A K 7 5 4
                        ♡ 7
                        ◊ K 9 5 2
                        ♣ A 10 2
```

West	North	East	South
			1♠
2♡	2♠	3♡	Dble
Pass	Pass	Pass	

Obviously South intended his double as a game-try, not wanting to commit his side unilaterally to game. But North read it as a penalty double and passed — with catastrophic consequences[1]. As you can see, North-South are cold for four spades but West succeeded in making his doubled contract, losing only a spade, two diamonds and a club.

The last hand was submitted to me for arbitration (not an enviable position). A Mexican expert was partnered with a visiting expert from South America.

These were their respective hands:

---

[1] North was wrong. Looking at jack-third of hearts, how could South have a penalty double? But more telling is that East's three-heart bid had taken away all game-tries. The logical countermeasure is to use three spades as competitive, and a double as a general game-try.

♠ 6	♠ A K Q 10 5
♡ A J 10 9 5 4	♡ 8
◇ K 9 5	◇ A Q J 10 3
♣ J 3 2	♣ A 4
Opener	*Responder*
M. Expert	*S.A. Expert*
2♡	2♠
Pass	

My Mexican friend thought the two-spade response was not forcing, so he passed without hesitation. The South American expert, irritated at having missed a laydown diamond slam (even the jack of spades dropped in three rounds), charged that his partner had no business passing a forcing bid.

Should he have bid a forcing two notrump and later presented his two suits? I leave it to you to judge. Incidentally, how would you bid these hands with your favorite partner?

My Tip for a Top

When playing with an unfamiliar partner:

Discuss the essentials of your basic system.

Treat every bid not specifically discussed as natural.

Keep it simple.

Don't try for the best possible result, but for the best result possible.

Chapter 2

Different Strokes for Different Folks

> Thou cutt'st my head off with a golden axe,
> And smil'st upon the stroke that murders me.

Romeo and Juliet, *William Shakespeare*

The following tip was suggested to me by an expert, with the proviso that his identity would not be revealed. I watched him playing in a major pair event with a good partner. This was the scenario when the final round came up: They were having an excellent game, but two good scores were needed for victory. Their opponents were a top expert, in the East chair, and an improving young player.

The first board produced a near top for my friend. Sitting South, he found a brilliant lead to defeat a seemingly ironclad contract.

This was the last deal:

```
Dlr: South            ♠ A J 10 8 7
Vul: E-W              ♡ 7 4 2
                      ◇ A 8 5
                      ♣ J 3
     ♠ 9 6 5 2                        ♠ 4 3
     ♡ K Q J 5                        ♡ 10 9 6
     ◇ K Q J                          ◇ 10 9 2
     ♣ ? 7                            ♣ ? 8 5 4 2
                      ♠ K Q
                      ♡ A 8 3
                      ◇ 7 6 4 3
                      ♣ A K 10 6
```

West	North	East	South
			1NT (a)
Pass	2♡ (b)	Pass	2♠
Pass	3NT	Pass	Pass
Pass			

(a) 15-17 points
(b) Transfer bid

The opening lead was the king of hearts. South could see that ten tricks seemed easy in spades. So the goal had to be ten tricks in three notrump.

With nine tricks on top, declarer planned to duck one round of hearts, win the heart continuation, run the spade winners, discarding three diamonds from hand, and take the club finesse. However, at trick two West switched to the king of diamonds. South had to change plans, ducking this trick too.

Now West returned to hearts, correctly leading the jack. Declarer ducked for a third time to rectify the count for a possible squeeze. This time, West elected to lead the queen of diamonds, declarer winning with dummy's ace. Immediately, he called for the jack of clubs. East played the two smoothly, South rose with the ace and West contributed the seven.

Declarer cashed the ace of hearts and his spade tricks. This was the three-card end-position:

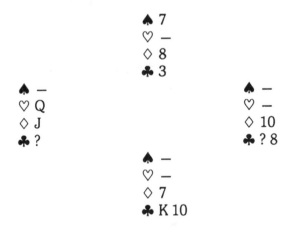

When the last spade was led from the dummy, East discarded the ten of diamonds and West the queen of hearts.

East had done well to keep two clubs, but South concluded that this East was good enough to do that even when not holding the queen. At trick twelve, he led a club to his *king* and dropped West's queen.

A well-earned top helped to ensure first place for the North-South partnership.

Afterwards, South said that against a beginner he would have had an awkward guess. He would be unlikely to retain a useless doubleton club; but also he would be unlikely to play low smoothly when the jack of clubs was led at trick four.

Try the next hand as a declarer-play problem.

```
Dlr: West                    ♠ 8 6 4
Vul: None                    ♡ J 4
                             ◇ Q J
                             ♣ A K Q 10 7 4

                             ♠ A 10 3
                             ♡ K 5 3
                             ◇ A 10 9 2
                             ♣ 8 5 3
```

West	North	East	South
1♠	2♣	Pass	2NT
Pass	3NT	Pass	Pass
Pass			

West leads the king of spades. You duck, win the second round of spades and cash your club tricks, coming down to this end-position:

```
                             ♠ 8
                             ♡ J 4
                             ◇ Q J
                             ♣ —

                             ♠ 10
                             ♡ K 5
                             ◇ A 9
                             ♣ —
```

How do you continue if West, who started with jack doubleton in clubs, has discarded, in order, (a) the eight of hearts, the queen of hearts, the six of diamonds and the seven of diamonds, or (b) the six of diamonds, the seven of diamonds, the eight of hearts and the two of spades?

   In the first case, it looks as though these are the remaining cards:

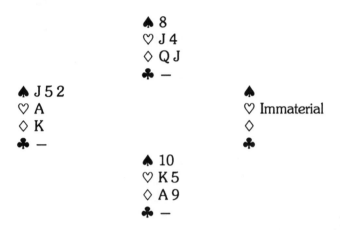

Probably, you led a diamond to the ace.

In the second case, it seems as though this is the situation:

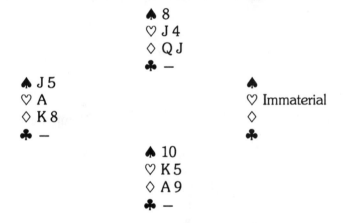

A spade exit will endplay West, forcing him to lead away from the king of diamonds.

However, against certain opponents this will not be true. In the first layout, the remaining cards will in fact be:

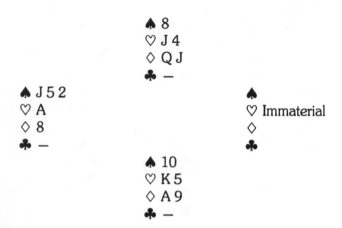

Playing a diamond to the ace does not bring any congratulations from partner, only from East for West.

Similarly, the second setup will be like this:

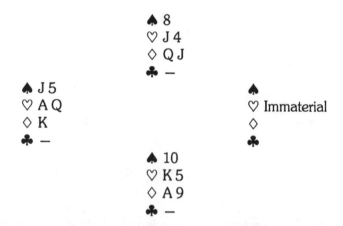

When you exit with a spade, West squeezes you with the final card in that suit. Once more you suffer an ignominious end.

One of the hardest aspects of bridge is this sort of endgame, where declarer can always make the contract double-dummy. But in the real world declarer's assessment of the play of the defender is all-important.

On the other side of the coin, the defender tries to give the declarer a losing option.

These hands provide several key lessons.

My Tip for a Top

Always size up your opponents; and watch their discards.

When you are the declarer: Duck tricks early to rectify the count. When a weak opponent discards an established winner, play him for the missing honor you are trying to locate. Be careful when drawing conclusions from the discards of expert opponents.

When you are a defender: Try to paint a different picture of your hand in the declarer's mind. Anticipate his plays. Make the critical discard early, not when declarer plays his last winner.

Chapter 3

ESP-N-E-1

If the doors of perception were cleansed everything would appear as it is, infinite.

A Memorable Fancy, William Blake

I am sure that all of my readers will be familiar with the acronym that ESP represents: extrasensory perception. With the abundance of science fiction books and movies, ESP, which is defined in the American Collegiate Dictionary as telepathy or clairvoyance, has found its way into our vocabulary.

You may be a believer or a skeptic, nevertheless the question is often raised: Does ESP exist at the bridge table?

Let me relate a stunning experience I had in 1978, at the Olympiad in New Orleans. Playing with my wife, Edith, I picked up this textbook hand for a weak two-heart opening bid:

♠ A 4 ♡ K J 9 7 6 4 ◇ 8 3 ♣ Q 6 5

As dealer with both sides vulnerable, I was all set to reach for the two-heart card in the bidding box when I suddenly got the eerie but overpowering feeling that six hearts to the ace-queen were sitting behind me. I tried to dismiss this presage as absurd, but it became stronger and overwhelming.

"Don't be ridiculous," I told myself. "With your scientific background, you certainly don't believe in such nonsense."

"You will see," an inner voice told me.

Fed up with this silent dialogue, I stopped in midair and ... pulled out the green "Pass" card.

I could hardly believe my eyes: My LHO opened with a weak two-heart bid!!

Since that time, I have been getting similar hunches or premonitions pretty often. Sometimes I get the foreboding that the cards are distributed in a certain way. I think the trumps won't break, or a key card is located in a specific hand. Or suddenly I get the warning that the hand I am about to pick up is a very difficult and delicate one, and disaster will result if I don't proceed with extra caution in the bidding or play. At the other end of the emotional spectrum, occasionally I feel strongly that nothing can go wrong, no matter what I choose to do.

I discussed this experience with a few of my expert friends, particularly those who are known for their unusual "table presence."

One of the finest players with this attribute, in my opinion, is Victor Mitchell. When I asked him about this topic, he said, "So what else is new? I have had the same experience for years. The air around the table is full of vibrations; if you have your antennae tuned, you can't help picking them up."

The late Barry Crane once told me that he firmly believed in streaks of fortune. Aggressive as he was, he increased the level of boldness if everything was running in his favor, with suits breaking evenly and finesses working. Then suddenly, inexplicably, he would feel the run had stopped and everything was turning sour, so he put on the brakes.

Is there an explanation? I believe that most of the players are so involved in their own problems (for example, trying to remember whether a bid is a sign-off, invitational or forcing, or finding the best line for dummy-play or defense) that they fail to observe or sense what is going on around the table. As they gain more experience their confidence grows and their "table feel" develops.

No chapter is complete without an illustration, so let me present a hand Marinesa Letizia showed me, which seems to confirm my point.

Dlr: North   ♠ 7 6 3
Vul: E-W   ♡ K Q J 10
          ◇ A K J
          ♣ Q 10 4

          ♠ A K 5 2
          ♡ A 9 7 6 4 3
          ◇ 8 2
          ♣ A

West	North	East	South
	1♣	Pass	1♡
Pass	3♡	Pass	3♠
Pass	4◇	Pass	4NT (a)
Pass	5♠ (b)	Pass	5NT
Pass	6◇	Pass	7♡
Pass	Pass	Pass	

(a) Roman Key Card Blackwood
(b) Two key cards and the queen of hearts

When Letizia bid five notrump, she announced that her side had all six key cards and that she was interested in seven. Her partner's six diamonds showed the king of diamonds and denied the king of clubs. Usually, showing specific kings will work better than just giving quantitative information as to how many kings are held.

The opening lead was the queen of spades, East playing the nine. You win, lead a heart to the king and cash the queen of hearts, East discarding the eight of spades. How do you continue?

There are two spade losers. Assuming the diamond finesse is working, one spade can be discarded. But what about the other one?

It looks as though West started with ♠ Q J 10 4. If so, you must play to squeeze him in the black suits. (This is better odds than hoping to find an opponent with king doubleton in clubs.)

If West has the king of clubs, you cash the ace of clubs, the Vienna Coup, run all the trumps, finesse the jack of diamonds and finish the diamonds to squeeze West. But if East has the king of clubs and West the jack, you must transfer the menace first.

A priori, it is better to play for West to have the king of clubs. This requires only one card to be well placed; whereas transferring the menace needs two cards to be well placed.

However, Letizia had a strong feeling that East had the key king. Backing her judgment, she played off the ace of clubs, crossed to dummy with a trump and called for the queen of clubs. East played low smoothly!

At this point, declarer had a sinking feeling. The percentage play, the simple squeeze, was going to work after all. Nothing for it now but to ruff and hope West had the king *and* jack of clubs.

Letizia did that, ran the trumps, finessed the jack of diamonds successfully and took the last two diamond tricks.

The operation was successful but the patient died as this was the full deal:

```
Dlr: North          ♠ 7 6 3
Vul: E-W            ♡ K Q J 10
                   ◇ A K J
                   ♣ Q 10 4
    ♠ Q J 10 4                    ♠ 9 8
    ♡ 8 2                          ♡ 5
    ◇ Q 9 6 3                      ◇ 10 7 5 4
    ♣ J 8 2                        ♣ K 9 7 6 5 3
                   ♠ A K 5 2
                   ♡ A 9 7 6 4 3
                   ◇ 8 2
                   ♣ A
```

Letizia couldn't believe it.

"Why didn't you cover the queen of clubs?" she asked her RHO.

"You led the queen of clubs because you wanted me to cover it. If you wanted me to cover, it had to be better for me not to cover."

Perfect logic!

If you have similar experiences, the obvious question comes up: What do you do about them? Do you trust such manifestations of prescience or do you dismiss them?

I can tell you it takes a lot of courage to back your hunches because if they turn out to be wrong, how do you explain to your team-mates or your partner that you took an unusual approach?

Over the years I have developed the following policy in dealing with this phenomenon: If I can get an exact, or even approximate, count on the hand, or the probabilities strongly favor one particular line (especially in team play), I go for it. But with either an understanding partner or all things being equal, I muster the courage and follow what the inner voice dictates.

My Tip for a Top

Make an effort to develop your table feel. When you have a relatively simple bidding, play or defense problem, try to concentrate on the vibrations around the table.

Believe in your hunches!

P.S. Don't try to hypnotize your partner to make a particular lead or play; it never works. Believe me, I have tried unsuccessfully a thousand times.

Chapter 4

Memory and Concentration

The Right Honourable gentleman is indebted to his memory for his jests, and to his imagination for his facts.

Speech in reply to Mr. Dundas, *Richard Brinsley Sheridan*

Early in 1989, I had dinner with my good friends Eddie and Bob Friedberg from Houston. As we had not seen each other for a long time, the conversation covered a lot of ground: family, health, hobbies, etc.

Suddenly Eddie remarked: "I don't understand one thing about Bob. His memory has worsened terribly. When I send him out for groceries he always forgets a couple of items on the shopping list, but when he is at the bridge table, not a single spot-card escapes him! Can you explain that?"

Of course, the answer is that memory and concentration are two different things. Related, yes; identical, no. Bob's memory may have worsened as it often does with age (I am sure he won't mind if I tell you that he is in his 80s), but at the table his game is as good as it was twenty years ago, outstanding at dummy-play and defense.

When having breakfast one morning during the 1989 Summer Nationals in Chicago, I discussed this fascinating subject of concentration, and whether it is possible to improve it, with Freddie Sheinwold. He was thinking of dedicating one of his articles to this intriguing subject. We decided to exchange our manuscripts before publication.

We agreed it would be best to deal with the case of the advancing competitor who wants to improve his concentration, and not with the aging expert or near expert whose attention span has started to diminish. It is impossible to reverse the physiological aging process as it leaves its imprint on one's once-superb memory.

I decided to start a poll among my expert friends, beginning with Freddie. The questions raised were this: Is it possible to improve one's concentration, and how should one go about it?

Freddie feels that it is easier to remember things in context rather than isolated facts. For example, one can memorize a poem much easier than the value of pi to the thirteenth decimal because words are related, numbers are not.

One of the most important moments in bridge is reached when the bidding ends and the opening leader tables his card. If the opening lead is an honor, it is generally easy to remember it; but if it is a spot-card, distracted declarers and defenders have great difficulty in recalling whether it was the three, four or six.

Freddie's advice is first to stop (which is a good idea anyway) and try to build a story around the opening lead. Try to relate it to the rest of the suit or to the opening leader's distribution. This makes it easier to recollect the exact number of pips on the card.

I go a bit beyond this. My suggestion is to write down the contract and the opening lead inside your convention card. Of course, the Laws forbid you to consult your card during the hand, but for many players the mere process of writing down the card led will help its subsequent recall. Whatever approach you take, everyone agreed that noting the precise card led to trick one is of paramount importance.

I think there are two kinds of people as far as memory is concerned: Those with a visual (or pictorial) memory, and those with an aural (acoustic) memory. For the latter group, I recommend repeating mentally: "The opening lead was the ... of ..."

I continued my poll by asking one of our top experts, a former World Champion. His answer, which I hoped would not be typical, was: "Gee, this is a very interesting problem. It is worth doing research in depth, but sorry I can't help you. I never had this problem."

Next, I turned to Mike Passell and Kerri Shuman. To my great surprise, they had similar answers: "You can improve concentration by self hypnosis!" Kerri added: "That's the way I learned to quit smoking, and it works for bridge too." She also said that it is not very easy to notice the declarer's first discard.

Almost all of my other interviewees stressed the importance of concentration. Ron Andersen put it this way: "When you sit down at the bridge table, you have to shut out everything distracting from your mind. You can't worry about family, finances, health or your job. The bridge table grows to fill the whole room, and your sole focus is on the cards and the opponents. It is an enormous effort, but it pays off."

"It isn't enough to concentrate; you have to know what to look for," was Edgar Kaplan's observation. "Most of the people learn how to count trumps, which is obviously important. But in the side suits few people know to remember the spot-cards and the order in which they were played. They place emphasis only on the fall of the high cards."

I have an amusing little story about this point, and I give it to you because it actually happened to me. In the mid 1970s, I played with Dan Morse in the final of the Blue Ribbon Pairs. My wife, Edith, was kibitzing. We were having a good game when an expert pair came to our table. On the second board, we had reached a bad six-heart contract on a 4-3 fit, when six diamonds was cold in a 5-3 fit. Somehow I managed to make my small slam.

After the hand, Edith turned to me and asked: "Did you see that?"

"Yeah," I replied, "what a waste of energy, to play in a 4-3 fit when every other declarer in the room is going to make six diamonds."

"No, I mean the girl," Edith continued.

"What girl?"

"The girl kibitzing your right-hand opponent."

"What about her?" I asked with a bit of suspicion in my voice.

"She was wearing nothing under her see-through blouse."

"What!" I exclaimed. "I am getting old. I didn't even notice somebody was sitting next to my RHO! Where is she?"

Smilingly, Edith pointed in the direction of the next table. At last I saw the blond buxom beauty. I expect that pair had a great game — unless my LHO could not concentrate on his cards!

Can you learn how to improve concentration? Here are a few valuable recommendations.

Edith Kemp Freilich: "I insist with my students that they pay great attention to the bidding, and, before the dummy hits the table, I ask them what they expect to find there. This is a great exercise, and at the same time it improves the student's visualization."

Eddie Wold: "Pick up five random cards and flash them for a few seconds to the student. Ask him to name the cards and the order in which they appeared. Then increase the number of cards, or alternatively decrease the time of exposure. Next, choose a suit from the deck and remove maybe two or three cards. Flash the incomplete suit rapidly before the student and ask him to name the missing cards."

Phillip Alder: "That is a good idea. Another approach along the same lines is to take, say, ten cards and lay them out. The guinea pig must name the cards in the correct order. Then give him other tasks for some twenty minutes or so. Finally, give him the ten cards again and ask him to put them out in the correct order.

"I tell all my students to remember the cards by saying every one to themselves. To name every card played, the person must have looked at each one. Not only does this make it more likely the key signals will be noticed, but also the actual cards played will echo in the mind."

Victor Mitchell: "Stress the importance of concentration, George. And here is another good exercise. Deal thirteen cards to the student and let him look at his hand. Count to five, and tell him to put the hand face-down on the table. Ask him to name every card. After repeating this a few times, the improvement in recall will become noticeable."

Try these drills for yourself and see how your concentration improves. Then you "only" need to carry it over to actual play at the table.

No final chapter is complete without a hand. My thanks for it go to my friend and multiple World Champion, Paul Soloway.

```
Dlr: South          ♠ A Q 8 4 3
Vul: Both           ♡ K Q 9
                    ◇ A Q 10 3
                    ♣ 6
      ♠ J 7 6                        ♠ K 10 9 5 2
      ♡ 7 4 3                        ♡ 6 5
      ◇ 9 7                          ◇ 8 6 5
      ♣ J 10 9 4 3                   ♣ A K 2
                    ♠ —
                    ♡ A J 10 8 2
                    ◇ K J 4 2
                    ♣ Q 8 7 5
```

At matchpoints, South became the declarer in a reasonable six-heart contract. Six diamonds is superior, but the lure of the higher-scoring contract was too great for South.

The opening lead was a devastating trump, the four of hearts.

Declarer won in the dummy and immediately turned his attention to the spade suit, hoping to find an opponent with king-third. He ruffed a spade in hand, then led a club.

West won and correctly continued with a second trump, again dummy winning. The ace of spades was cashed, a club being discarded from hand, and a spade ruffed. No luck; but our declarer did not give up. He ruffed a club in the dummy and came back to hand by overtaking the ten of diamonds with the king. South drew the last trump and played the jack of diamonds, overtaking with dummy's queen. This was the three-card ending:

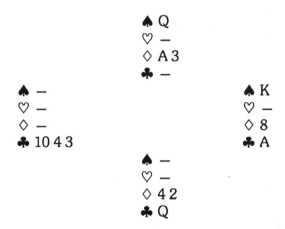

Declarer cashed the ace of diamonds and played the four from hand. Now came the three of diamonds. What was declarer's final diamond? After a lot of thought, East guessed wrongly and our hero made his slam.

Soloway did not mention the declarer's name, but judging by the play I would not be surprised if he were sitting South.

Just before finishing, let us consider one other thing that is detrimental to concentration: jet lag. If you will need to be mentally sharp after a long journey, try to arrive one day early for each one-hour time zone crossed. Also, if taking a particularly lengthy trip, try to arrive in the late afternoon or evening. You will want to sleep, and you will get back into rhythm that much quicker.

I hope this final chapter will stimulate a lot of interest in the topic; and I expect to receive some mail from different quarters.
    In the meantime, here is:

My Final Tip for a Top

If you think your concentration at the bridge table is fading, don't blame it on bad memory.
    At the table, try to shut out of your mind everything not related to bridge.
    Follow some of the recommended exercises to enhance your concentration.
